WAKING UP
CHASE

ONE STUDENT'S JOURNEY TO AWAKENING HIS POTENTIAL

By

Darryl Bellamy Jr.

Waking Up Chase Copyright © 2013 by Bellamy Inspires, LLC

Bulk Sales

Books are available at special discounts for bulk purchase. For more info email Info@BellamyInspires.com.

Interested in making Waking Up Chase as a required campus read? Contact Bellamy Inspires, LLC to learn about special college/university editions.

Cover design by Emir Orucevic
Book design by Saravanan Ponnaiyan

ISBN 13: 9781530437924
ISBN 10: 153043792X

First Edition: March 2016

DEDICATION

This book is dedicated to the student who
does not know the way,
is currently searching for the way,
or is well on their way.

This story was created for you.

PREFACE

I remember searching through multiple books, looking for one that offered what I felt a college student needed to know. Not having much luck, I decided to start writing. Over a year and a half ago I sat down to write what I felt you needed to know in order to thrive. My goal was simple, to stop your future regrets; to get you to take advantage of everything undergrad offered, so when graduation ends, you're running off campus!

I started writing the first chapter of a "How to" book, sent friends a draft, but the excitement soon faded. As weeks of no writing turned into months, it became clear I wasn't taking the right route. Luckily the feeling didn't last long.

The story of Chase and his journey came after reading one Sunday evening and once he entered, he wouldn't leave. The plot and characters flooded from all directions and unlike my first attempt at writing, I couldn't stop once I started.

Chase is like most students, trying to find his or her way in the complex undergrad ecosystem. He is new to campus, information is bombarding him from all angles, and he is not sure what route is the right one. 'Waking up Chase' is compiled of many lessons I learned during my years packaged in an intriguing story. I pray this will provide some guidance on what I know will be a prosperous journey.

Meet You at The Top!
@BellamyInspires
#WakingUpChase

TABLE OF CONTENTS

If you don't read this book once it is given to you.
If you don't apply what is within, the story will become you.
Don't take this lightly and don't ignore.
For those who do have a great adventure in store.

— PART —

1

THE BEGINNING

1 THE ARRIVAL

Stuffed in an over-airconditioned SUV with my younger siblings and everything I could possibly fit in for the year ahead, the feeling is definitely there.

You know, the feeling of excitement with a slight edge of apprehension? The feeling you get when you are about to embark on something new, or out of your comfort zone.

Or should we be more honest and say the feeling of not really knowing what would become of this year. Actually, let's forget about this year for a moment, how about not really knowing what the next four years would be like!

Will I make friends?

Will college be easier or harder?

What will the parties be like?

Do people really drink as much as they do in all the movies I watched?

…and last but not least, is the guy to girl ratio skewed?

The answers to all my questions, only time will tell.

I had a good set of friends in high school, but who says my social skills would translate to college life? I would describe myself as an average student because I did average academically. By average I mean not terrible, but nothing to rave about.

At this point my parents are just happy I got accepted somewhere. I wonder what is going through their minds now as they sit up front, their heads bobbing slightly to each beat on the track. My bet is they are yelling and cheering inside!

It's funny because as soon as that thought runs through my mind, I look at my mom and catch her face shifting to a smirk - as though she's thinking about something happy. She's organizing what she plans on doing with my room back home I bet. Dammit, I think to myself, she IS cheering inside!

Let's talk about high school for a moment. All throughout high school I heard my teachers say "In college this" and "In college that"…

They loved saying what a college professor would or wouldn't accept. I would come a little late to class sometimes to hear, "A college professor is not going to accept that". A college professor probably couldn't care less in a class of 300+, I would say under my breath.

My teachers loved giving advice, but I evaluated everything they said with a little something called "common sense." What did they really know anyway? Most of them haven't been in college in over ten to fifteen years, some more than that. What do they really know?

I did my research. I've read a few articles online, watched a few "Things you should know about college" YouTube videos, and even read a few Buzzfeed lists to get a feeling of the upcoming years ahead. Not to mention I skimmed a few college prep books I received as graduation gifts. Trust me, I'm ready.

Freshmen Orientation also gave me a good idea of what to expect, but by now I've come to the conclusion I'll just have to experience what college is for myself in order to understand.

"*How long dad,*" my younger sister yells to my dad driving.
"*30 minutes,*" he says back.
"*Is Braden there yet?*" my mom turns back to ask me.
"*He arrived about uh week agooo*" I reply, laughing at myself.
"*Actually, he arrived an hour ago,*" I say, correcting my previous joke, knowing it had gone straight over her head.

2 MEET CHASE

If there was one person my parents trusted more than me, and believe me there's probably a list of folks, it would be Braden.

Braden has been my best friend since sophomore year of high school. We get along well because he knows how to have a good time. Anytime we're together, you can be sure it's not going to be boring.

My parents love Braden because he's the kid every parent wants their kid to hang out with. Braden is responsible, except for when he was with me of course! He was also overly involved in high school and naturally smart. The type of smart that can look at an assignment once and immediately get it. Yeah, that was Braden all right!

He could also get away with anything because no one would ever suspect him. Me on the other hand, all fingers were always pointed my way.

If I were being completely honest, I would have to admit that Braden kept me out of trouble multiple times! So when it came to choosing a school, there was no other option but to not only attend the same school, but to room together.

I reached down and grabbed my phone...

"Thirty minutes till FREEDOM!!" I text Braden.
"Hell yeah, man!" he responds.
"How does our room look?" I ask.
"Nice size for a good party...Lol," he shoots back.
"AYYYE, be there in about 30 minutes brosky," I type.

I knew with Braden as my roommate, this year was sure to be epic! I'm thirty minutes closer to my freedom. The freedom to not have to answer to my parents or follow their rules for curfew. I'll finally be able to make my own decisions.

To say my parents are overbearing is an understatement, but I still found a way to have a good time. They insisted on me being home by a certain time, showing them certain school assignments and meeting my friends and their parents. They wanted to be able to control almost everything I did. Not anymore they won't! I'm ready to finally take control of my own life.

My parents also wanted me to be involved in extra curricular activities in high school, but I enjoyed spending my time with my friends after school instead of wasting time in club meetings or volunteer activities. I joined a club junior year for resume purposes, did the least work possible and hyped it up in my college essay – WIN! You know what I mean?

My goal for my next four to five years is simple, go to as many classes as I need to in order to pass, enjoy the parties and alcohol, and take full advantage of the guy to girl ratio!

The thirty minutes my dad mentioned earlier had gone fast, I notice the college entrance coming up ahead.

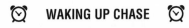 **WAKING UP CHASE**

2 $\frac{1}{2}$ MONTHS LATER

"Y'all still going out tonight?" I ask my boys as we throw a ball back and forth across the room.

"*Chase, you have a 9am tomorrow, you know that's a bad idea*" says Braden

"*He'll be alright,*" the others chorused, trying to convince me to come along. Of course Braden had to be the one to offer up the logical aspect of everything. But maybe I wasn't trying to be logical tonight.

Two months into this thing called undergrad and I can say I've adjusted well. Finding friends wasn't as hard as I thought it would be, as all incoming freshmen are searching for friends during the first few weeks. I hadn't considered how we would all be in the same predicament, you know? All on the prowl for a new set of friends.

As far as classes are concerned, those are going alright. We just took midterms and I'm praying I did ok as this grade could tank me if I didn't.

"*Watch out!*" Jake yells as the ball we're throwing hits the lamp on Malik's desk and pushes the lamp onto the floor with a crash!

"*Shit!*" he says as he starts cleaning up what looks to be a million pieces of glass all over the floor. As Malik throws the pieces in a half full trashcan, our RA Steven walks past to see what all the commotion is about.

"*What's going on?*" Steven says, bending down and attempting to assist picking up pieces of broken glass.

"*We were tossing the ball......and it......*"

As Steven is helping with picking up glass, I notice his eyes turn to something underneath the desk and he reaches forward to pick something up. My gut wrenches in slow motion, as I pray it is not an old alcohol bottle or something worse!

Uh, oh I think to myself, not knowing what caught his attention, as I wait for him to pull out his find.

Luckily for us, it was only the book all students were given during Orientation. We were also given a few assignments in our College Seminar course, but they were all easy assignments to BS without actually reading the book.

We got through the assignments without reading the book, but RA Steven would not let it go. For some reason he lived by the book and would always ask us if we read it yet. You would think the author was paying him to make sure students read it. When he picks it up, we all look at each other, shaking our heads, knowing exactly what's coming next – another speech. ☺

We knew he was about to be at it again, as he stood, wiping off the dust the front of the book had accumulated underneath the desk.

"*I know y'all were SUPPOSED to read this for class, but how many of you ACTUALLY read it?*"

We all look around for someone to raise their hand. Out of the four of us, only one person raises their hand and you can probably guess who it was…

yup, Braden.

Steven continues on his rant, which we've heard in different forms…multiple times, since Day 1 on campus.

"*It's important that you all read this and not skim it,*" he continues, "*as there could be consequences out of your control if you don't.*"

As he says that, he and Braden gave each other a weird look. Not sure what it means, but it is as if they know something we don't. Like there's a check or something at the back of the book for everyone who reads it.

"*This book was pivotal in my success,*" says Steven, who was now a junior and very influential on campus. He also mentions how he's decided to run for Student Body President this spring and would like our assistance with campaigning. "*I would be a different student if it wasn't for this right here,*" he repeats, as he holds up the book.

What Steven didn't understand about me was, if I got through the class assignments without reading it, I wasn't going to read it now. I haven't got involved on campus yet and I don't really see the point now, I am comfortable. My boys and I have great laughs and we are satisfied as we realized that College Only Happens Once, so we should enjoy it, right? - COHO!

Braden was always pressuring me to "get more serious" as he would say, or to "join this or that organization." There is one thing I know for sure, I made it through his attacks in high school so I figure I can ignore him for another four years without any issues.

CHAPTER

4 THE PRE-GAME

As I get dressed to head out for the night, I realize how the guys always get me to go out when I've originally said no. They always make the same arguments…

Jake's favorite saying is "YOLO" which stands for you only live once and Malik would always throw out "You won't get another undergrad experience." Both statements were true, but I also wanted to GRADUATE from my undergrad experience!

One thing I can say with certainty is my friends help me live for today instead of always focusing on the future, and not enjoying the present moments. Too many people are always over-planning and never enjoying life.

I was glad Braden decided to come along as our 'DD' for the night, which he only did because his first class didn't start until 12:30 tomorrow afternoon. Either way, we always had someone in that position every time we went out. One thing we all agreed on was that one person not partaking in the drinking that night to ensure we got home in one piece was worth all of our lives.

"*Where are the shot glasses?*" asks Adrian as he closes the room door and brings his bottle out from the back corner underneath the bed.

"*Shots, Shots, Shots, Shots, Shots, Shots!*" we all chant as we take a few and put on some music before heading out to the car.

Who knew the pre-game would be one of the last things I remembered from that night...

— PART —

2

CHASE AWAKENS

CHAPTER 5

FORTY MINUTES TILL ELEVEN

I feel my head pounding and the sunlight beaming on my face as I begin to wake up from what had to be an epic night by the way my head is feeling. With my eyes still closed, I gently reach for my comforter, desperate to pull it back over my head, while silently cursing God for creating the sun.

As I grab for the comforter I hear…

"You only have forty minutes till eleven o-clock."

Realizing I've already missed my Thursday 9am class and feeling the hard effects of last night, I'm not the least bit concerned about anything Braden wants me to do this morning. He should be getting ready to head out to his 12:30, as he likes to get breakfast and then arrive early to claim his front row seat in class.

I turn over to drown out his voice, which sounds like he too had a hard night; I open my eyes gingerly to see some unfamiliar posters on the wall.

Hmm, I think to myself, I don't have a these posters by my bed. Slowly, I begin to wake up.

"Eleven is getting closer!" says Braden

"Shut up Braden, I'm not going to class. It's not happening today," I say back in frustration.

"Wow, it was that sort of night?" Braden asks.

I start to become confused the second time Braden speaks, as his voice sounds much deeper than I recall. I slowly sit up in my bed to notice the room looks familiar, while also very unfamiliar.

Dammit, I think, where did I end up?

As I look around, I notice the room layout is the same. I am still in Moore Hall, but everything has been updated. The walls have a fresh coat of paint, the furniture is more modern, and there's carpet on the floor where there was once old tile. There is no way they could have renovated our room in one night! My mind is spinning in a hundred different ways.

I look down at the comforter, which is definitely not mine, and then to my shorts, which happen to be sporting my rival NFL team - I would not have been caught dead in these, not even for sleeping. This HAS to be a joke from the guys. Idiots.

Something is definitely off, I'm still thinking to myself, as I look around the room.

I know Housing and Residence Life were in the planning process of renovating this residence hall, but that wasn't scheduled for a few more years. How were all the renovations made so fast and how did I end up here? Who's room is this?

⏰   **WAKING UP CHASE**   ⏰

I continue to scan the room as though I have been endowed with some sort of spidey sense, noticing that nothing I see looks like mine. As I continue to scan the room…

I turn towards Braden's side of the room and see an individual looking back at me.

Who? An individual, that's all I can tell you. I can't give him a name, as I have no idea who he is! That would explain why I thought Braden's voice sounded deeper!

I quickly scoot back towards the wall in shock, now facing the individual head on. If I had to choose between fight or flight, I just went into flight, but I'm only about two seconds from fight!

"Who the hell are you?" I say, staring him down.

The guy gives off a light chuckle as if to say I should definitely know who he is.

"That hard of a night?" he asks, laughing.

I immediately start thinking about the previous night…pre-game, shots, nothing.

Damn, trying to think harder.

Went out with boys, I remember the pre-game, talking to people when we arrived…uhhh, blank. I'm pissed; I should have listened to Braden and stayed back.

I quickly grab my phone while keeping a watchful eye on the guy sitting on the bed across the room.

As I grab my phone, I quickly spot that it's not my phone, but it's an iPhone nonetheless so I click on messages to find anything to jog my memory.

I scroll through contacts to see nothing familiar; my phone must have been gotten switched last night by mistake! This phone looks like an iPhone, but a newer version, one I haven't seen before.

"*Crap,*" I say aloud, not recognizing any of the names.

Pictures – that's it! Clicking through the app I start frantically scrolling through the photos but there's no-one I recognize.

"Are you ok?" says the guy on the other bed.

"Are YOU ok?" I say sarcastically as I quickly jump out of bed and hurry to the mirror near the sink.

As I reach the sink, I turn on the cold water and start to drench my face. I obviously didn't turn on the right faucet, as the water comes out steaming hot! I turn that faucet off and turn on the other one. As I look up into the mirror, I'm immediately taken aback by what I see. So stunned that I literally jump back and jam my spine on the dresser behind me, causing me to become even more frustrated!

The guy starts laughing; I look at him with a glare as his laugh turns back into a silent confused stare.

As I look in the mirror, I see a guy looking back at me that looks nothing like me. My mind starts racing, what the hell is going on, what happened to my face? Where am I? Who is this guy? My heart starts beating faster.

As I look at the guy in the reflection staring back at me I see clear differences. My hair is cut shorter, ears are smaller, and my eyes are no longer the light brown they once were. Not to mention all the other facial differences.

It doesn't take a rocket scientist to figure out that the person I see in the mirror is not me.

REFLECTION

What if you awakened in an unknown place and couldn't recgonize yourself? How would you be thinking and feeling?

6 CHASE MEET AIDEN

Actually, this guy is CLEARLY not me! The guy I see looking back at me in the mirror is the same guy I noticed in the phone, which I guess should give me a little bit of comfort - I guess.

I pinch my arm, thinking this is the time to wake up – NOW!

Nothing happens.

I try the water on the face trick, but again, nothing.

Ok, unfamiliar room…check
Guy I don't know…check
Updated iPhone, not mine, but with pictures matching the guy in the mirror…check

I turn to my temporary roommate… *"This is going to sound really weird, but who am I?"* I asked as I start looking for a weapon in the room to defend myself, just in case he's playing some weird creepy game.

"Who are you?" he asks back with a chuckle.
"Yes, who am I?" I insist, still not laughing. ☺
"Are you asking me what your name is?" he says.
"Yes, that too," I say, now starting to get angry.

"Not sure what type of time you had last night, Aiden," he says.

"Aiden?" I ask.

"Aiden Clark," he replies, still looking confused.

Who the hell is Aiden Clark? I think, digging through college memories; Aiden Clark, Aiden Clark? I don't even know an Aiden, let alone an Aiden Clark.

Noticing my confused and bewildered look, my roomie starts to explain.

"You're a freshman at Myatt University. You enjoy watching ESPN and you know everything imaginable about college basketball. Your major is engineering and by the looks of how you're acting right now, you can't handle your liquor," he laughs.

Again, I look at him not laughing back, I just stare. I figured he would have picked up on the context clues by now.

"What's your name?" I ask.

"You're acting very weird, man. My name is Mason. Are you sure you were ONLY drinking alcohol last night?" Insinuating I may have tripped out on something else

"Why are you acting so weird this morning man, are you alright?" he asks again.

Aiden? I think to myself, who is Aiden?

"Any other questions CRAZY Aiden?" he says, half laughing, half serious. "See, I told you not to go out drinking the night before meeting your senior mentor!"

Did he just say senior mentor? Meeting? What is he talking about? Nothing else Mason said this morning was comical until he uttered the words *"meeting your senior mentor."*

I would never sign up for a mentor, besides I wasn't doing terribly to need one! Signing up for something like that is something Braden would have done. I made it through high school ok, why would I need assistance from a mentor now?

Nothing but idiots wasting time talking.

"Senior Mentor?" I finally ask Mason.

"Do I have to remind you of everything?" Mason says, sounding a little like Braden with that statement. I can't get rid of a friend that thinks he's my parent no matter where I go.

"Chase is coming by to pick you up at eleven," says Mason.

"Chase who? Me Chase?" I ask.

"No dummy, your name is Aiden, not Chase, You wish you could be that guy…"

He continues.

"Campus leader, Student Body VP, sound familiar? You're lucky to have gotten him as your mentor, everybody wanted him. Don't F this up man" says Mason, sounding like he was one of "those people" that wanted him.

⏰ **WAKING UP CHASE** ⏰

Finally a piece of information that makes a little sense but makes absolutely none at the same time. Maybe Mason was right; I start to think I might have consumed more than alcohol last night too.

"Mentor, as in he's going to be giving me advice and help?" I ask.

"Don't ruin the opportunity you have today to learn everything he learned his last three years, it would really be a waste," says Mason.

I think hard, Chase mentoring me today? Now I'm royally confused.

"Take good notes Aiden, I got stuck with the President of the Math Honor Society, I'm sure I'll need your notes," pleads Mason.

We both laugh at the same time, picturing what his mentorship day will be like. The more Mason talks the more I'm able to put pieces together and make sense of my situation.

Knowing my past, I knew the Chase he was speaking about couldn't have been me or connected to me in any way. I always felt I was destined for something, but definitely not at the level this Chase guy he mentioned had reached.

"What's his last name?" I ask.
"Markham," Mason responds.

Dang, why was I secretly hoping this Chase didn't have my exact same last name?

Maybe this guy was me after all? Same first and last name would be more than just a coincidence. I went to the desk on the side of the room I woke up on, and opened up Facebook to type my name "Chase Markham."

As the profile appeared, I was floored!

This Chase guy was clearly me, but an older looking version. When I say me, I'm talking about the guy I was yesterday, not this Aiden character. He had more facial hair, looked a lot more mature and seemed to have achieved a lot by all the accolades on my profile. He even has the abs I always wanted – WIN!!

Scrolling to the date in the corner of the MacBook I notice the year is not current. I click "Date and Preferences" and click "update" as the year seemed wrong, but nothing happened. The date stayed the same.

"Uhhh Mason, what year is it?"

He responds with the same year on the Mac, which was four years ahead of what it was yesterday.

"Ok," still thinking…Now things are starting to make a little more sense to me, well not making sense but this would at least explain the updated iPhone and the renovated room. That would also explain the older looking me I just saw on the profile.

Where am I? Have I been thrown four years ahead?

Yes. Somehow between last night and today I've come forward four years, but not as myself. As I stand there looking through my pictures on my profile, certain moments start coming back into memory.

⏰ **WAKING UP CHASE** ⏰

THE STORY BECOMES YOU

I start to work my way backwards, going through as many memories as I can possibily remember. As I scroll through Chase's pictures I can't help but think about the look Steven gave Braden after he asked us about the book he found under the desk.

Did the look they gave each other have something to do with this? Did they have an idea that something like this could happen?

I remember him holding up that book given to all students during Orientation, but what was it about? I tried to think harder…thinking about the first few pages I flipped through when I opened my bag during Orientation and scanned it for class.

As I think back, I remember a few words from a poem in the front pages,

"If you don't read it once it's given to you, something, something like something will become you."

No, no, not it! Trying to think harder.

"If you don't read it once it's given to you, something, about applying something will become you?" Darn, getting even more frustrated, wishing I had read it in class.

THE STORY WILL BECOME YOU, that's it! "If you don't read it once it's given to you, if you don't apply what's within, the story will become you!"

"Hey Mason," I say looking over at him, *"do they still give out that book to every incoming student at Orientation?"*

"Yeahhhh, didn't you get one? Why you ask?" he says.
"Where is your copy?" I say, ignoring his question.

He points to his bottom desk drawer. I open the drawer, going through mounds of papers and supplies until I finally find it. I open it up and flipped straight to the front.

> If you don't read this book once it is given to you.
> If you don't apply what is within, the story will become you.
> Don't take this lightly and don't ignore.
> For those who do have a great adventure in store.

Holding the book up, *"You read this?"* I ask Mason.
"Yeah, good story and tips in there," he responds.

After turning to the back cover of the book, I finally realize what has occurred. The look Braden and Steven gave each other now makes perfect sense – bastards!

"Damn," I say repeating the last words aloud *"don't ignore, for those who do, have a great adventure in store."*

8 DIGGING DEEPER

Thinking about what I saw on Older Chase's profile, there is no way that could be my future. Especially being the guy I was yesterday.

You know, the no extra curricular activity, looking for a good party, doing juuuuussst enough to get by Chase? Yeah, that guy.

Still confused at what was occurring and how this Chase became who he was, there was only one way to find out - meet bruh myself.

I glance down at my watch to see the time is 10:50 a.m. The Chase I knew yesterday would definitely be late to pick me up, but I'm sure the one I've been stalking online would be on time.

With ten minutes to go, I quickly throw on a set of Aiden's clothes and wait for Chase's arrival while continuing some last minute social media creepin'. At three minutes to eleven, my phone vibrates and there was only one person it could be.

I look down at my phone to see my name. My name never looked so good!

Chase: *"Downstairs, come on out man."*

"On my way down," I reply as my heart starts racing with anticipation. As I head to the elevator to make my way downstairs, I start considering my game plan.

Alright, you're going to have to tell him, I say to myself. No! Bad idea, just play like Aiden the entire day, says the other voice, fighting with the first voice in my head. I start laughing as I remembered my middle school teacher saying "It is perfectly ok if you talk to yourself as long as you don't answer back."

I'm answering back. This is a problem.

I wipe my palms on my jeans as I head out the door towards the car in the distance. Who would have thought I would be nervous about meeting the person I understand the best - myself?

"You got this, you got this!" I say, pumping myself up to get rid of any nervous jitters as I head straight for the car parked in the roundabout out front.

REFLECTION

How would you feel if you were about to meet your future self. What feelings would you experience? Would you be excited, nervous, scared?

CHAPTER 9

MEETING MYSELF

Upon getting closer, I immediately notice my 2008 Nissan Altima. It looked a lot better when I had it, but it is almost four years older now. I was hoping I would have had a better car than that by now, but I guess we don't get everything we want, right?

As I approach the car, Chase steps out and around to greet me, looking just like the social media photos. I can't help but be amazed at how much I've grown up!

"Hey, my name is Chase," he says, reaching out to give me a firm handshake.

"Hey, I'm Aiden Claaarrrrrk," stuttering a little as I remember the name Mason told me earlier.

"Nice to meet you Aiden" he says, as we open our doors to get in the car.

As we start driving with my favorite artist playing through the speakers, I can't help but feel really weird. Not just the normal weird I usually feel, but the type of weird you can only experience if you're sitting next to someone that looks just like you. I now know how identical twins feel every day of their lives...probably not.

Every opportunity I get, I try to ask Chase a question, trying to find out as much as I can about him to support my suspicions.

"Why did you choose this school?" same reason I did.
"What high school you go to?" same.
"Any brothers or sisters?" same.
"Hobbies?" same.

Every question also gives me the opportunity to turn and look at Chase as I try to look for as many similarities as possible.

After one question, Chase clearly caught me staring.

Great, I say to myself, he thinks I'm a creep.

My mind is still shooting every which way; I'm amazed and shocked all at the same time! How did this happen? How did I get here?

I remembered pinching myself earlier, but this time might be the charm! I move my right hand towards my left arm to create the appearance as though I'm about to scratch, but instead I gently pinch myself. If this is a dream, let's go ahead and wake up…come onnnnn!

Nothing happens.

Music still playing in the background while Chase is still telling me about his interests, which I know all too well because they are mine also.

Chase is still talking as I pinch myself again, this time a little harder.

Shit, no luck, I say under my breath.

"Huh?" he says, looking at me confused.
"Oh, nothing," I say back quickly.

As we talk about our friends, the only name I recgonize is Braden. I wonder what happened to all the guys I hang out with now - I think, where did they go?

After telling me about MY family and MY interests, he finally starts inquiring about my life.

"So, tell me about yourself Aiden. What do you like to do?"

"Well," slipping over my words, *"we actually have a lot in common..."* as I name the same artists and interests he did earlier.

He pauses for a moment while glancing at me with a confused expression. His look is as though he feels I am just copying him and am not unique or something.

Again, my mind is racing and I'm not sure what I should do. I should have thought through these potential answers in the room.

Should I tell him who I am...or should I just go through the day normal?

Will he think I'm crazy?

Will he kick me out the car?

Well, I've already weirded him out, so I have nothing to lose. As he starts asking more in depth questions about who I am, I take a deep breath and...

"Hey Chase, this is going to sound weird…"

Chase looks at me as though I'm about to profess my love to him or something. I can see I still haven't learned to stop showing all my emotions on my face!

"Yes?" he says looking over, *"feel free to share anything man, I'm here to help in any way that I can."* Not truly meaning what he says.

"Well," I said, *"last night I was drinking with some friends and I blacked out."*

"That's all right man, no reason to feel bad, I remember those days," Chase says with a slight chuckle.

"Well, there's more," I pause, *"I didn't wake up in my room this morning either."*

"My man!" he yells, reaching out to give me a high five!

"No, not quite Chase, I wish!" I say.

His face turns to one of bewilderment.

"I didn't just wake up in a different room, but it seems as though I've come forward about four years in time."

"In time?" Chase asks, still confused as a condescending laugh escapes from him. A laugh that signals him asking himself, what the hell did I get myself into and how did I get assigned this nut job as a mentee?

"So you're a ghost from Christmas past?" he says with a laugh, trying to laugh off my previous statement.

I look at him without laughing. ☹

"So, tell me about who you were before you blacked out?" he asks while he figures out how to protect himself from this nut job in his car.

"Well, that's the thing" I say, bracing for the worst.

"What do you mean?" asks Chase.

"Yesterday, I was a younger version of you, Chase." Voice slightly shaking.

"Of me?" he queries.

"Yes, of you."

Chase pauses for a moment and turns the Altima into the next parking lot we pass.

Oh shit, I think, this is about to get real!

Chase slowly turns into the parking lot and parks, turning to me as much as he can in a vehicle.

"So you are saying that you are a younger version of me?" he says, looking me straight in the eye, hands together on his lap.

"Yes. Last night I was hanging out with Braden and a few others..."

He interrupts, *"My best friend Braden?"*

⏰ **WAKING UP CHASE** ⏰

"Our best friend" I respond. *"I seem to have blacked out and woken up as this Aiden guy. No clue how it happened."*

"So you expect me to believe that you were me yesterday? Am I being Punk'd?" he says as he looks around the car and parking lot for cameras, looking frustrated.

"No, you're not being Punk'd," I assure him.

Chase takes a deep breath and starts laughing. It wasn't a happy laugh, but a weird one. It couldn't be described as mad either. All I can say is, it was weird. *"Braden must have put you up to this...How much did he pay you? Prank of the century!"*

"I promise Chase," I say as if I'm pleading to a jury, *"this morning was as weird to me as it is to you right now. I promise I'm telling the truth, pinky swear!* I hold out my pinky towards Chase.

Chase looks down at my hand, *"Did you just say pinky swear Aiden?"*

"Yeah," I say, realizing I just said pinky swear.

"You're a grown ass man Aiden, don't you ever say pinky and swear in the same sentence ever again in your life, ok? That's your first mentorship lesson of the day," he says sarcastically.

"If you're really a younger version of me and you 'woke up' here this morning, prove it!" says Chase, 25% of him trying to believe me and the other 75% thinking I'm full of it.

"Prove it?" I ask.

 WAKING UP CHASE

"Yeah, prove it!" he demands, looking me in the eye.

I didn't expect him to ask that and I quickly start thinking back to a moment only I would know, something I've never shared with anyone. If I'd never shared it with anyone, that would mean Chase wouldn't have shared it either. I start going through life's past moments from childhood on forward and even past secrets in my head. *"Got it!"*

"You went to West McKinley middle school, right?"

"Yes I did, or should I say "we" did" says Chase sarcastically.

"You remember how much fun we had in 5ᵗʰ Grade? You remember the class council we created?" I ask.

"Yeah sure," he says, still not believing me.

"Now do you remember when you took Charlotte's homework out of the homework basket to copy because you didn't finish yours?"

"What are you talking about?" Chase says, still denying the fact that he did it, a small smirk forming on his face.

"What does that prove?" he asks.

"Do you remember how you forgot to put it back in the homework basket and when Mrs. Evans handed out the graded copies, Charlotte didn't get hers back. You recall her being upset when Mrs.Evans didn't believe she turned it in?"

⏰ WAKING UP CHASE ⏰

Chase lets out a small laugh *"ha ha,"* knowing he never told Charlotte he took it and no one ever suspected him of doing anything of the sort.

"You never told anyone that you took it out and you definitely never told Charlotte you forgot to put it back," I remind him.

"Sounds familiar?" I ask.

Chase looks at me in disbelief. Disbelief because he never told anyone and it was a secret he held to this day.

"I'm not sure why we held on to that as it wouldn't hurt us at this point, right?" I say to Chase as we both laugh.

After laughing and sharing other stories for a moment, though apprehensive at first, Chase became a little more comfortable after reminiscing....He turns to me with a smile, holds out his right hand for a second time and says...

"Nice to meet you, Chase."

"Nice to meet you too, Chase," I reply, taking a deep breath of relief.

REFLECTION

What moments, memories, or secrets would you share and discuss with a future version of yourself?

— PART —

3

TIME WITH
LINDA

10 THE DAY

"*What's our plan for the day?*" I ask as we drive towards the center of campus.

"*Today we're going to meet a few people who made me into the student and campus leader I am today. I have to find ways to up the anti now that I know I'm mentoring a younger version of myself. I don't know why or how long you're here, but I'll be sure to give you everything I can to ensure we are a success,*" says Chase

"*Thanks, I'm not quite sure why I'm here either but I'm along for the ride,*" I reply.

"*If you were anything like me in freshmen year, I know exactly why you're here!*" Chase says, laughing. "*I wouldn't be who I am today without the stuff and people you're going to meet today, so pay attention so we can ensure our future success. Can't have you eff'n it up.*"

We park at what is a new parking deck on campus and start our walk into the center of the campus grounds. As we walk, Chase catches me up on some of the cool things that occurred over the past few years. I am amazed to see the amount of growth and the continued beauty of the campus in such a few years.

Half listening to Chase as he's giving the tour on the way to our first destination, I still can't wrap my head around how he has become so successful. The way Mason described him this morning, he was THE man on campus, well liked and a student leader. Not to mention all I read about him online.

Mason was right. As we walked through campus we were stopped every few minutes by a wave or a quick conversation with someone else Chase knew. I noticed how Chase always used names when greeting those he came in contact with and how everyone who left his presence left with a smile.

"How do you remember everyone's name, Chase?" I ask as we continue walking.

"Good question, Aiden. I learned early on that a person's name is the sweetest sound to their ears. Remembering someone's name is a way of showing that they matter to you."

> **"** *A person's name is the sweetest sound to their ears. Rememberinging someone's name is a way of showing them that they matter to you.* **"**

"That's powerful," I reply, considering how good I feel when someone I only met on a few occasions remembers my name.

Who would have known that one day I would be dropping knowledge like that? I always knew I had potential, I knew I was smart, but I was comfortable just getting by. I would have never imagined this type of success in a hundred years. I knew I would find out in detail how Chase became Chase, but my impatience wouldn't allow me to wait any longer.

"Hey, Chase" I say.

"What's up?" he replies.

"I'm perplexed with how you became such a leader on campus and accomplished everything you have thus far. If I look at my life yesterday, I wasn't on this track." I continued explaining, *"At this point in my first year, I'm not doing great and though I'll probably graduate, I don't think my senior year will look anything like yours."* I paused. *"Looking back, what was your turning point? What made the difference?"*

"Ha-ha," as he laughs, ever so slightly.

"There's a lot I can name, but there was a catalyst. Remember the book that was given to all incoming students? You know the book you're living now, whether you know it or not?"

"Yes, I think that's whats happening," I say sarcastically, but still very much unsure.

"I came into college just like you, relying on my past negative actions and thinking those same actions would get me through college successfully," says Chase. *"After reading the book, I decided I wanted to at least attempt to be a better individual and leave a legacy on this campus. I didn't want to keep repeating the same mistakes and expecting different results – if you know what I mean?"*

> **"** *Insanity is doing the same things over and over
> expecting a different result.* **"**

"Yeah, I understand," I respond guiltily.

Chase continues, *"When I got the book, I decided to read it and apply it to not only my college experience, but also my life. I took notes and applied the information I learned."* He laughs, *"Not to mention the front poem about the consequences of not reading scared me a little."*

I laugh as well.

As Chase continues, I start to feel like I wasted time. Here I had all the knowledge I needed in front of me to take the first step, but didn't take advantage of it. It reminded me how many times we look everywhere for a solution, when the solution is right in front of us.

REFLECTION

**What solutions are you searching for when the answer
is right in front of you?**

Chase looked over and could see the disappointment on my face. *"The great thing about today is I'm going to show you everything I learned from the book. If you listen to what I teach you and ultimately apply it, I have no doubt with the brain you have, I mean the brain we have, you will be successful."*

"How do you know what my brain is like?" I ask jokingly.

"I just know," he says as we both laugh.

"You're almost one semester down, but you still have ample time to make a pivot," says Chase.

As we arrive at the career center door, Chase turns to me and looks me in the eye. *"By the way, I'm not the older you, I'm the potential you."*

He pauses to let it sink in.

"What do you mean?" I ask, not fully understanding what he means.

"I'm not the older you, I'm the potential you," he repeats.

"Explain," I say.

"Everything I have accomplished over the last four years is NOT guaranteed to you, but you have the potential to achieve all of it. Your success will be determined by how well you apply the knowledge you learn today, for knowledge without application is useless."

He lets that sink in as we enter our first location.

Wow, I think. He's right, I'm staring my potential right in the face, literally. I immediately wrote down "Your potential is available to you, but not promised to you."

REFLECTION

In what ways are you living or not living up to your potential in this current moment?

⏰ **WAKING UP CHASE** ⏰

CHASE TIP

As you continue reading, be sure to underline, highlight, circle and make note of anything that catches your attention. I'm taking notes throughout today so I can apply this later; I want you to be able to do the same.

CHAPTER

11   MEETING LINDA

*"**H**ey Chase!"* said the woman at the front desk as we enter the office.

"Hey!" we both respond as the lady gives me a funny look. Chase elbows me in the side.

We walk past the front desk and down a hallway lined with offices. The walls of the hallway are lined with pictures of students and different campus landcapes.

"Today I want to introduce you to my Career Advisor, Linda. She's full of so much knowledge regarding navigating college and beyond," Chase says as we make our way down the long hallway.

As we turn into the office, an enthusiastic voice bellows out *"Hey Chase!"* as she comes around the desk to give him a hug.

"And you must be Aiden?" she says, putting her arms around me in an embrace. Her energy and passion flow from every part of her being.

"Yes ma'am I am," I say politely.

Her office is filled with different Student Affairs awards as well as pictures of her with successful students. The office is filled with color, from the carpet underneath the desk to the color portrait of the school mascot behind her desk. If you wanted to be a winner, I can tell she was the one to get you there.

Right beside her desk is a stack of books and on the other side of her office is a bookshelf lined with even more books. I can't keep my eyes from wandering as my attention is constantly grabbed by something else of interest.

She ushers us to a small table with a few chairs adjacent to her desk.

"So, Aiden, you get to hang out with this guy all day, huh? I told him to be nice to you," Linda said, smiling.

"Yeah, he's been good thus far," I said with a chuckle as Chase gives off a slight laugh.

"I wanted you to meet Linda as she was one of the first people I met on campus and has made a big impact in my life." says Chase.

Linda blushes slightly, *"You put in all the work Chase, I just did a little guiding along the way."*

"Aiden, tell me about yourself," Linda demands, not wasting any time.

As I start to make up things about myself to share with Linda, I notice a blank sheet of paper in the center of the table. It isn't just because it's a blank piece of paper that it catches my eye; it's the fact that it is laminated. I continue talking until I notice one similar with words hanging on the wall behind Chase's head.

"Linda, what is that?" I ask, stopping in the middle of my introduction and pointing to the laminated paper. I'm also trying to change the subject after making up everything humanly possible about Aiden's background.

Chase smiles as though he knows there is a clear answer to the question. With the smile still on his face, he turns to Linda.

"Well, that right there Aiden, is whatever you want it to be…"

says Linda.

"Whatever I would like it to be?" I respond, puzzled.

"Correct," she says.

I had a feeling where she might be going with this, but was still confused. Linda slid the laminated paper over to me. Now it was closer, I could see that the paper had words typed on it. It looked as though it was a blank resume of some sort.

The following words were on the page:

Name

Degree

GPA

Job Experience

Leadership/Activities

Awards & Recognition

"Every student, especially new students that schedule an appointment with me, is given one of these laminated blank sheets," Linda says.

 WAKING UP CHASE

Chase chimes in, *"If you understand this one sheet, it will make a huge difference in your life four years from now. This one sheet has been crucial in my college progression."*

"All I see is a few words with blank space," I say, looking at them and then back at the paper.

"Exactly," says Chase as he continues, *"It's up to you to fill in the space."*

I start thinking that this day might be a waste of time; I came four years into my potential future and walked all the way across campus just to be shown a blank laminated resume?

"What's important about this sheet is…it doesn't care," says Linda.

"Huh? It doesn't care?" I question.

"Exactly, it doesn't care Aiden," Linda says.

Well duh, I think to myself, it's a piece of paper!

Linda continues, *"The sheet doesn't care who you used to be in high school, this sheet doesn't care about your high school friends, GPA, sports teams or anything else you've accomplished in the past. It doesn't care if you got voted Prom King or most likely to not succeed. The only thing this paper cares about is what you do from Day 1 on this campus."*

"So many students start college, not stopping for a moment to realize they're able to either build on their solid foundation from the past or become the person they weren't in the past. It's totally up to them to decide who they want to be."

Chase chimes in. *"Not sure what type of student you were in high school Aiden,"* he winks, *"but I wasn't involved, I didn't take my academics seriously and extra-curricular and leadership positions were not my main concern. I just wanted to have good time without worrying about anything else."*

"Similar to me" I say, looking back at Chase.

"It's ok to have a good time in college," Linda says. *"Actually, we want you to have a great time while you are here, but three years from now you will have to hand this paper to future employers. Will you hand it over with pride or will you hand it over the same way it sits on this table?"*

She pauses, *"Blank."*

> ❝ *Will you hand it over with pride or will you hand it over the same way it sits on this table?* ❞

At that moment I start thinking about all the limiting beliefs I let ride along with me to college. Limiting beliefs I had about my past that I'd brought along with me into my freshmen year. The thoughts that said, I didn't do well in high school, was never the best at academics, so why try now? Or the voices that said I made it into college without getting super involved in high school so why couldn't I do the same thing again?

I never for a moment considered that the actions that got me to where I am now, might not get me to the next place in my life. I assumed it would, but we all know what happens when we assume, right?

> ❝ *What got you to where you are now, might not get you to where you want to be in the future.* ❞

Seeing Chase sitting across the table fully opens my eyes to what's possible. I start to become discouraged as I realize that I've been playing this semester and myself small. I think about how I haven't been putting in the work I should have, based on negative thoughts and experiences from my past and those limiting beliefs. I begin to think about my circle of friends, and how we are living so small compared to what we could be accomplishing.

Linda spoke up, *"Aiden, college is TRULY a new start. Your GPA is new; you're around a new set of people that might not know who you USED to be. I have known many students that weren't the best in the past, but made a pivot when they realized the importance of their fresh start."*

"Don't mess up your fresh start," she reiterates as I sit quietly, taking in all she just said.

> ❝ *College provides you with an opportunity to start over, don't mess up your fresh start.* ❞

"Ok, I understand we get to start over, but how do we fill that paper? How do we start?" I ask Linda.

"I'm about to show you how," she says.

12 FUTURE VISION

*"***A***iden, have you considered graduation day?"* says Linda.

"Yeah, I planned on graduating," I say as they laugh.

"No, Aiden. Have you played that day in your mind?" she clarifies.

"Like, what will be your GPA? What friends will be around you for pictures? What leadership positions would you have held? What memories would you cherish?"

"Have you ever considered that day?" Linda asks.

"No, not really," I say.

Linda continued, *"It's important to have a glimpse of the future in order to get on the path to making it happen."* She continued with a confident voice, as though she wanted me to take it in. *"By looking forward and feeling those feelings now, it's easier to take action and start making your plan. Too many students just fly through their years, never once considering the end goal.*

"I want every student who works with me or anyone else in this office while at Myatt University to have some sort of vision about graduation

day and their future from the start of college. I want every student to leave college without having to look back."

"You don't want them thinking about their college experiences?" I ask.

"No, silly. You should always look back on your college experiences with pride, but not with the wanting to go back. There's a difference."

She pauses as I let it sink in.

"Those who want to go back and experience their college days all over again, usually didn't do much while they were there," Linda says and both she and Chase laugh.

"You will never hear the students who were successful during their college years, say 'If only I could go back to college again.' That statement is saved for those who coasted through and didn't leave a legacy."

"Why wouldn't successful students say that?" I ask.

"You won't hear successful students say that because they left it all on the table. They gave everything they could give while on campus, so even if they were given the opportunity to go back they wouldn't because they gave it all. In short, they left empty.

"Aiden, I want you to leave empty," she says.

"If you do it right, everything you do in college will set you up for such a good post grad life that going back to college would be a set back."

Chase nodded in agreement and added to Linda's comments.

"Sometimes I catch up with some of my friends from freshmen year and I hear them talking about how they wish these times would last forever. Now don't get me wrong Aiden, my college experiences have been great, but I'm using my college career as a set up for a future of great experiences. Why would I want this to last forever when I have a future of new experiences ahead?"

66 *Your college years should not be the best years of your life. Your college years should set you up for the best years of your life.* **99**

Chase continued, *"The only reason they want these times to last forever is because they aren't prepared for what comes next."*

I had been wondering about what happened to all the friends I used to hang out with, Chase's comment prompted me to make a mental note to inquire more about their whereabouts later.

Linda spoke up *"I personally remember having so much pride and excitement on graduation day as I walked across the stage many…many… MANY years ago."* We all laugh.

"I remember being surrounded by family and taking pictures with the friends I'd gained over the years. I also remember feeling a sense of peace, as though I'd given everything. I also recall an intense feeling of satisfaction knowing that I gave my all. I was involved on campus, I took advantage of opportunities and I started early filling in those sections," she points at the paper framed on the wall behind Chase's head.

Take a moment to envison your graduation day. What friends and family will be with you? What have you accomplished?

"*The earlier you start the better off you will be in the future. That goes for maintaining a good GPA, getting involved on campus, and taking advantage of all the resources this campus offers you.*

"*You ever wonder why we have only 15 Career Counselors for thousands of students?*"

"*Why is that?*" I ask.

Linda replies, "*It's because the vast majority will never step foot in this office. Everything doesn't have to make sense for you to start doing something. You want to start now with what interests you and go from there. Inaction or not doing anything at all is never the answer.*

"*Future employers are no longer asking questions like 'What are your strengths and weaknesses?' They're now asking questions like 'Tell me a time when... and describe a situation when...'. If you weren't involved on campus what situations are you going to describe?*"

❝ *You want to start now with what interests you and go from there. Inaction or not doing anything at all is never the answer.* **❞**

⏰   **WAKING UP CHASE**   ⏰

"It all makes sense," I say, my mind still racing from all they just said.

I continue on... *"I just always thought that those leading organizations or those with good GPAs had some supernatural talents that I didn't have, that's why I never attempted to get involved or make my GPA a priority."*

"It's obviously in you," Chase says, pointing to himself, forgetting that Linda doesn't know about our morning mishap.

I jump in and comment before she notices what Chase did, *"The thing y'all said about starting with the future and working backwards makes sense as I want a job out of college, but I have to have something on paper to show I deserve the opportunity, right?"*

"Exactly" said Linda as she finishes up.

"You have talents and skills that make you unique and special compared to others. What saddens me is how many students realize this too late. Start preparing now Aiden. Start now, you'll be glad you did." She slides the laminated paper all the way over to me. *"That's for you,"* she winks.

"Schedule an appointment with Beth at the front counter on your way out. After you fill this out we can start planning on getting you to the top," she smiles. *"The fact that you signed up for a mentor is the first step, and being assigned to Chase was even better. I'm not going to hold you up too long. As Chase said, you two have a full schedule today."*

She turns to Chase, "Where to next?"

"Lunch with The Cabinet," he says.

⏰ **WAKING UP CHASE** ⏰

"Ohhhhhh…The Cabinet," she grins. *"You're going to have a great lunch Aiden."*

"What makes them so special?" I ask sarcastically.

"Well for one, they've all sat at the same table you're sitting at now," says Linda.

"Ok, makes perfect sense," I say as we grab our belongings and head towards the door.

"See you both soon," says Linda as she reaches out and embraces us both.

"You know it!" I say excitedly, wanting to see her again, but not knowing for sure if I will have the opportunity.

REFLECTION

"A goal not written is only a wish."
Take some time to write down a few things you plan to accomplish before graduation. Complete this before moving forward.

Name:

Degree:

GPA: Let's aim for 3.0 or above _____

Job Experiences: What job experience will you showcase?

Leadership/Activities: What are you involved in or what organizations would you like to join? How will you lead in these organizations?

Awards/Recgonition/Certifications: Being recognized by your peers is one of the highest forms of praise. This section will provide proof of your results to employers or graduate programs.

13 FIND YOUR GUIDE

*"**D**id you get all that?"* Chase asks as we walk out the front door and back outside into the fall air.

"Yeah," I said, *"I hadn't realized how important it was to visualize the future and work backwards. I never took the time to think about what I wanted and how I wanted to feel; therefore the motivation was never there for me to make it happen. It is as though I was walking blindly expecting to get to my final destination."*

"Remember," says Chase, *"even though the blind can't see the same way we can, they still have something guiding them. It may be a dog or a walking stick, but they're still guided by something. You need to decide what you're going to be guided by over the next few years."*

"Touché," I reply, *"Touché."*

> **"** *You need to decide what you're going to be guided by over the next few years.* **"**

I start to envision my parents proudly standing around me, along with my younger siblings who have come to see their older brother graduate. I visualize myself having a job offer before the end of my senior year and being the type of student leader Chase was, so students would be hyped about being my mentee.

Chase interrupts my thoughts. *"When I arrived at Myatt I thought I could be successful by myself. Meaning without regularly going to advising appointments, finding someone on campus like Linda or someone else to have my back. The truth is, it's possible, but it's not ideal. It's important for all of us to have someone to hold us accountable, even Oprah Winfrey and Bill Gates have coaches and mentors.*

> **"***Everyone needs someone to hold them accountable.* **"**

"For you Aiden, it maybe a professor in your major, or a club advisor, for me it's Linda. Find someone you can talk with openly and honestly, who is behind you and can offer support and guidance. You want someone who's not afraid to tell you the truth. When you try to go about it alone, it takes you longer to find your solution and you start making mistakes you could have advoided. Think about the stories mom and dad always tell, they're not trying to run our lives, but prevent us from making the same mistakes they made. Take advantage of the wisdom from those that made mistakes before you so you don't have to repeat them."

We continue walking through campus.

REFLECTION

Think about those individuals currently in your life. What wisdom can you gain? Who is your support system, how do they guide you positively?

CHAPTER 14 PUT ON YOUR MASK

"The Cabinet" I say, punching Chase in the arm as if I was Pacqiuao. *"How did you come up with that?"*

"Damn, that hurt man" clutching his arm.

"Are you familiar with the Presidential Cabinet? You know the people who head all the different agencies in the US government?" asks Chase.

"Of course, I remember that from US History in high school," I say.

Chase explains, *"My close group of friends call ourselves The Cabinet as we all lead different organizations on campus."*

"So all of our friends are student leaders?" I ask.

"You mean, my friends?" he says, laughing. *"I know who your friends are."*

"Yeah, all of your friends, I guess," I say.

This brought me back to what Chase said earlier about visiting his friends from freshmen year, and how he didn't mention any of the friends I have now, except for Braden.

"Chase, what happened to the friends you used to hang out with in freshmen year, you know the ones we spent all our free time with?"

"You mean Jake, Malik and Adrian?" he asks.

"Yeah, what happened to them?" I say.

"Well, Jake is no longer in school and I still hang out with the rest every once in a while, just not as often." he says.

"Where is Braden?" I ask, wanting to see him before the day is over.

"Oh, he's stuying abroad this semester," says Chase.

"Dang," I say, mad I'm missing my opportunity to see what the potential Braden is like, but not forgetting Chase no longer hangs out with Malik and Adrian as often as he used to.

Getting the feeling Chase has changed, I call him out. *"Oh I see… once you got involved on campus and became a big time student leader you just left your old friends behind huh? Doesn't seem too loyal to me,"* I say with a slight laugh, while being serious.

Chase looks at me and smirks, as though he knows this is going to be a teachable moment.

"Aiden, do you remember when we went on the family cruise during the summer before our sophomore year in high school?"

"I do", I replied, not knowing what a family vacation had to do with any of this.

WAKING UP CHASE

"Remember when we were on the plane headed to Florida before we got on the boat to sail to the Caribbean?"

"Yes," I replied (wanting him to get to the point).

He continued, *"Before the flight took off, the flight attendant gave safety instructions to all the passengers. She said if the plane were to experience a drop in altitude, the oxygen masks would drop, and we were to put on our own masks before assisting others. You recall that?"*

"Yes, but what does that have to do with you not hanging out with our original group of friends?" I ask impatiently.

"Give me a minute," Chase says as he continues with his story. *"The flight attendant was instructing us to ensure we could breathe properly before assisting others with their masks. If you did the opposite, you might find yourself not breathing permanently,"* he laughs.

"Yeah I get it," I said quickly.

Chase continues, *"Too often, we hold on to friends that might not be the best influence because we're attempting to help them breathe. We're always attempting to help them out of their problem, when we can't breathe ourselves because we never put on our own masks."*

> **❝** *We're always attempting to help them out of their problem, when we can't breathe ourselves because we never put on our own masks.* **❞**

⏰ WAKING UP CHASE ⏰

"Freshmen year, after I read the required reading and visited Mrs. Linda, I came back to our friends pumped to share the knowledge and epiphanies I learned that could help us dominate on campus. Everyone besides Braden laughed it off, blew me off and wasn't serious in making changes. After having a clear vision of what I wanted, I couldn't let their small thinking stop me from achieving what I wanted for my 'blank sheet.' I decided it was time for me to put on my oxygen mask before helping them put on theirs."

"So none of them were interested in making a change?" I asked.

"They were too comfortable with the lives they were living. Think about it, we hung out around campus, no real responsibilities, partied whenever, who wouldn't want that life?" says Chase.

"Yeah, we do have some epic times," I murmur to myself, while going through a few in my head.

"Aiden what would happen if you kept assisting someone in putting on their mask when they didn't want it on in the first place? They would keep taking it off, and you would spend all your time worrying about their life when they're not interested in saving it themselves. Sometimes you have to wait for them to experience such a drop in altitude that they're fighting to put on their own mask."

> **❝** *Sometimes you have to wait for them to experience such a drop in altitude that they're fighting to put on their own mask.* **❞**

"WOW, that's good!" I say to Chase. All this time I felt it was disloyal to separate myself from those who held me back, especially since we've been friends for a while and we've shared certain past experiences. But, the breathing metaphor makes it clear, if they're not willing to put on their own mask, I have to ensure I can breathe by putting on my own.

Chase continues, *"If our old lifestyle produced extraordinary success I would still be spending time living that lifestyle today, but the people I wanted to emulate lived differently. Let's be clear, they weren't terrible people or doing terrible things, but they also weren't living up to their full potential. I wanted to push myself to see what was possible if I tried. In short, our friends were living exactly how you are living now, doing just enough to get by."*

"Dang, that hurt!" I say, grabbing my gut as if someone has knocked the wind out of me

REFLECTION

Consider your group of friends, are you holding on to their masks when yours is still hanging from the ceiling? What next steps can you take to make sure you can breathe?

"Remember this," Chase says. *"Small-minded students look at the limiting of interactions with people that are preventing them from breathing as being a disloyal friend. Successful students realize that it's the only way to ensure the potential success they strive to reach.*

WAKING UP CHASE

"Studies have shown time and time again that we are the average of the five people we spend the most time with. If you spend time with five student leaders, I guarantee you'll be become the 6th student leader. If you spend all your time with five alcoholics, at some point you WILL become the 6th."

"Uhhh, how could that be true?" I ask.

"It's has been found to be true with salaries, net worth, and even body weight of friends. People rub off on us whether we want them to or not. One thing we all seek, whether we admit it or not, is to fit in with our peer group."

"If your peer group consists of all student leaders, imagine what their conversations are about. If you spend your time with them, you have no choice but to assimilate in order to fit in. Next thing you know you're joining an organization, figuring out how to lead so you have stories to share the next time you're with your friends."

Not completely sold, I had to question Chase further. *"I don't totally buy this notion of friends rubbing off on us. You are saying I have to separate myself from my current friends? You're also saying my friends' mindsets will rub off on me even if I'm really focused and motivated and they're not?"*

Chase answers, *"Let's be clear, I'm not telling you to do anything. I'm offering what has worked for me and all those I know to be successful. Remember, all this knowledge is yours to do with what you wish. I want you to think about your friends and surroundings as air quality. If you work out, eat right, and live a healthy life, but live in a city with terrible air quality, you're overall health is still being affected. Right?"*

"Right." I say.

"I still go back and hang with them or go to a party with them every once in a while, but I don't spend all my time with them, as it will impact my breathing capacity," says Chase.

I laugh, as this breathing metaphor starts making sense.

"Let me get this straight," I say, looking at Chase for confirmation.

"I want to ensure my mask is on, before assisting people with putting on theirs, especially if they are not interested in putting their mask on for themselves?"

"Correct," Chase says.

I continue, *"You are also saying that surrounding myself with those who do not have similar goals can harm me, even if I am really focused?"*

"Yes, your surroundings affect your air quality. It's not your job to stay around people who are not interested in living up to their full potential. Consider this, as soon as you help one friend with their mask, another one takes theirs off, it's a continuous cycle. They keep taking theirs off in rotation, because they never wanted to breathe in the first place! They take it off because they were never interested in putting in the work to be successful. You want to surround yourself with people who can not only put on their own mask, but also keep it on while helping others. Kinda, like I'm doing for you now," says Chase.

> **"** *You want to surround yourself with people who*
> *can not only put on their own mask, but also*
> *keep it on while helping others.* **"**

"I can breathe fine," I say to Chase.

"You have the future potential to breathe fine," Chase says, *"it's all about…"*

"Application," I say quickly as if I'm a contestant on a game show.

"You're catching on man, you're catching on," Chase says with a smile.

REFLECTION

Consider the five people you spend the most time with.
Are they helping or hurting your average in different
areas of your life?

— PART —

4

MEET THE CABINET

15 PERSONAL RESPONSIBILITY

A s we enter the Student Union and head to the second floor where the on-campus restaurant is located, the smells of food immediately hit me. After all the information this morning and no breakfast, this Aiden guy is ready to eat! We enter the restaurant and immediately head into a private room on the left.

Why are we passing the food? Let's get my food and then meet these people I think to myself.

"I see y'all with the private room!" I say to Chase. *"Y'all run this campus I see!"*

"No, we know how to reserve a room," Chase says back jokingly.

As we enter the private room located at the back of the restaurant, I see six individuals sitting at the table awaiting our arrival. *"Everyone, meet Aiden,"* Chase says. The group immediately crowds around to greet me and introduce themselves.

They are all a part of a few organizations so they choose to only mention their most important title. I feel welcomed from the first hug; I wonder why everyone I meet today is a hugger. I wonder if hugging is in "the book" also.

The six individuals in The Cabinet include:

Bryan - President of Campus Activities Board
Chase - Student Body Vice President
Imani - President of PanHellenic Assoiation
Reagan - Student Body President
Zach - President of Campus Athletics Association
Braden - SGA-Chief of Staff (studying abroad)

Also included at lunch was Bryan's older brother Steven. Chase introduced him to me as a former campus leader who graduated two years ago and was one of the original founders of The Cabinet. He didn't have to introduce his brother Bryan, as he was the first one I recognized when I entered.

The energy in the room was electric. How could people have so much energy? Chase seated me right in the middle of the rectangular table, with direct access to everyone.

"How has your day been so far?" asks Bryan, Head of Campus Activities Board.

"Full of information" I say. *"My head is about to explode!"*

"I wanted you to meet some of my friends who are student leaders on campus so you're not stuck with my thoughts all day," says Chase.

"Thank God for that," Reagan chimes in as everyone laughs.

"Do you have any burning questions for us Aiden?" says Reagan.

I thought for a few seconds and went with the first question that came to my mind. *"Actually I do. If you could name one thing that made you successful these last few years, what would it be?"*

They all turned to each other to see who would answer first.

Imani, who was the Council President of the PanHellenic Council, spoke up.

"If I had to pick one, I would say a positive mindset and taking responsibility for everything that happens in my life," Imani says confidently.

The table's noise volume immediately rose with an *"Ahhhhh,"* as everybody looks around the table, wishing they had said it first.

"What do you mean by mindset?" I ask, looking at Imani. *"I recalled Linda talking about the importance of my first year and thinking about what I want in order to make it happen, but I didn't recall her mentioning anything about mindset."*

Imani answered, *"Mindset is how you look at life's situations, those around you, and also how you control what happens to you."*

"So how has that helped you?" I ask.

"Did you read the required reading?" she asks *"No, not yet"* I reply. At this point I was tired of hearing that book mentioned. I knew when I got back, if I got back, I had to read it.

"Well, you'll hear this again when you read that book along with the second book that goes into greater depth on all the concepts. The second

book came out sophomore year, right?" she asks, and the group nods in agreement.

"But the section on mindset shifted my thinking and altered the way I looked at college. Let me ask you a question," she says, looking directly at me.

"Have you ever not done well in a class?"

"Yes, this semester actually" I say without a pause.

"Why are you not doing well?" she asks, as everyone stares at me, waiting for my answer

"Well this particular class is taught by a professor who has a strong accent, making it hard for me to understand. The class is also an 8am class, making it even harder to attend. I would be doing a lot better if it wasn't for that."

"So, whose fault is it that you didn't do well?" says Imani.

"I'll take a portion of the blame, but the majority would be placed on the professor and the department. If I could understand the professor better I would be doing better hands down!" I say confidently.

"Whose fault is it you are not doing well?" she asks again, obviously not hearing what I just said.

I started thinking of more reasons…

"Oh, I forgot about the 8am timeframe. My Orientation leader recommended I take that professor during Freshmen Orientation and the only time it was offered was 8am. So part of it was her fault also."

 WAKING UP CHASE

The entire Cabinet laughs at my last answer.

"What???" I ask, not understanding what was so funny.

"I'm glad we get to meet you today Aiden, because right now you're about to have your mind blown!" says Imani as she continues…

"There is one major thing that will stop you from being a mediocre student and allow you to succeed these next four years and even in life; and I'm going to share it with you."

I sit up in my seat, waiting for this epiphany from Imani.

She continues, *"There is a clear difference between students who perform on a high level and those who barely get by. There is also a difference between those students who leave college fulfilled and those who always want to go back to their undergrad years. It can be summed up in two words,"* she continues, *"Personal Responsibility."*

Personal Responsibility? That was the one thing? That was the mind-blowing information? I am in disbelief.

Zach, sensing my confusion speaks up. *"When Imani asked you who was to blame for not doing well, you took a tiny piece of the responsibility and immediately shifted the rest of the blame."*

Imani took up the thread again, *"If we look at most campuses in the world today, the students who are stuck are usually in that predicament because they don't take responsibility for what occurs in their life. They are always searching for something or someone to pass the blame to. In order to be successful during your academic career and life, you must take responsibility for everything that happens to you.*

⏰ **WAKING UP CHASE** ⏰

"EV-ER-Y TH-IN-G", Imani says slowly.

> **"** *In order to be successful you have to take personal responsibility for EVERYTHING that happens in your life; everything is your fault.* **"**

"Here's what most miss: you only have control over that with which you take personal responsibility. You can't control a professor's accent, you can't control how someone teaches, and sometimes you won't be able to control your class times. The one thing you always have control over is how you respond to all those situations."

> **"** *The ONE thing you always have control over is how you respond to everything life throws at you.* **"**

"You said everything?" I ask for clarification. *"Do you honestly mean everything, even those things I have no control over?"*

"You're thinking about this all wrong Aiden. You have control over everything that happens to you, whether you know it or not. The easiest thing to do is shift blame. I've seen countless students blame bad professors for receiving certain grades, blame roommates for certain issues in their room, blame their parents for things that happened in their lives. Some students spend their entire lives blaming everyone around them for everything that's happening to them."

REFLECTION

What things in your life are you shifting the responsibility/blame to others for when you should take full responsibility?

"Here's the key," Imani continues. *"You ONLY have control over what you take responsibility for."*

She pauses.

"You might not be able to change the situation or person, but you can always control how you react. As long as someone else is to blame you will always be in the…" Imani looked at everyone else for a response.

Without hesitation, everyone shouted out *"Victim stage!"* The entire Cabinet said it together, as though it was a group motto or something! My guess is that it was probably written in "that book" everybody kept talking about.

"In order to move from the Victim to Victor stage you have to take responsibility for EVERYTHING that happens in your life and know there is always a way out and a reason for it occurring," says Imani. *"When you are blaming others you are a victim, when you take responsibility for what you can control you are now a victor."*

> **"** *When you are blaming others you are a victim, when you take responsibility for what you can control you are a victor.*
> *Choose to be a victor.* **"**

 WAKING UP CHASE

Reagan chimes in, "*Sophomore year, I remember a particular teacher that all the upperclassmen warned me was a bad professor. They said she didn't teach well, and didn't really care if you did well. It was something to do with tenure, which you'll learn about later Aiden.*

"My first question to them was, did anyone in the class get an A? The response was and is always a yes. The upperclassmen responded that the people who got As were this and that, and super smart along with some other excuses. To which my response was, if at least one person got an A, then someone found a way to overcome the obstacles and succeed, therefore I could too, with enough dedication. To be honest, even if no-one in the class got an A, it's still possible. In life you either find a way, or fade away."

"In life you either find a way, or fade away."

"It is soooo much easier to fade, so most take that route. If you noticed Aiden, I never debated the professor's teaching ability, because the professor's way of teaching is not in my control. I can't control her teaching, but I can control MY response to her teaching. I only focus on what I can control, and I go from there.

"The easy route will always be to give up and stop looking for solutions, but there is always a solution for every issue. You might not like the options presented because it involves you stepping up, but there is always a way!"

> 66 *You might not like the options presented because it involves you stepping up, but there is always a way!* 99

"Here are a few examples, Aiden" says Chase.

"You can't control your class time, but you can control what time you go to bed the night before. You can't control your professor's accent, but you can control whether you get a tutor or go to office hours."

Chase continued, *"If you blame the professor, your grade will always be out of your control. Shifting blame is the quickest path to mediocrity."*

> 66 *Shifting blame is the quickest path to mediocrity.* 99

"When you take personal responsibility, your mind shifts to finding a solution instead of looking for reasons to blame for your non-success. Take responsibility for everything that happens in your life, no matter what it is."

"Agreed wholeheartedly," says Steven, who graduated two years ago. *"The same thing is true for the work world as well. You won't always have a boss or employer you love, but you have to realize that you are always in control of yourself. I have co-workers that blame my boss for anything that occurs at work, whereas I take personal responsibility for everything and was recently promoted."*

"*Congrats,*" says Chase to Steven, reaching out to give him a high five!

"Aiden. Everything you're learning now will translate over to your post grad life. Time and time again, those who blame others don't move forward, because they will always be in the Victim stage and never rise to the Victor Stage. The world is full of victims."

I looked at my life and considered the long list of things I shifted to others, when I should have taken responsibility. I imagined what life would be now if I had realized I was in control the entire time.

"*WOW, it's sort of freeing, knowing I can take control of any situation by first taking responsibility for everything that occurs in my life,*" I say with a smile, understanding the concept and its meaning.

"*Let's try this again,*" says Imani.

"You're not doing well in a class, who's to blame?"

"*Me,*" I respond.

"You don't get a certain internship or job you want, who's to blame?"

"*All me,*" I respond.

"*Good,*" she says.

"*Let's step it up a notch. If someone you don't know comes into this room and punches you in the face, who's fault is it?*" she asks, while The Cabinet laughs.

"It's mine" I respond.

"Why is it your fault or why should you take responsibility for someone you don't know punching you in the face. That sounds kinda stupid doesn't it Aiden?" she says with a sarcastic laugh.

"No it doesn't," I say confidently. *"Because as soon as I shift the blame to that idiot, I no longer have control over the situation and I remain a victim. By taking responsibility for any and everything that happens in my life I can then figure out what I need to do to change the situation or prevent it from occurring again."*

"You got it," says Imani, *"you got it!"*

Chase looks over at me with a proud smile, knowing I fully understand, and my future will be different because of it.

REFLECTION

Imagine your life if you took responsibility for everything that happens to you. How will your life look different in 1, 5, or even 10 years from now if you did?

Now, Imagine your life if you continued to live in the victim stage, 1, 5, 10 years from now. Do you like what you see?

CHAPTER 16

THE NUMBER FOUR

Chase looks over to Steven.

"Steven, you've been out of school for about a year or more now, right? Any advice you can offer the group?"

"Hmmm," said Steven, *"There's always something, I just gotta think what would provide the most value."* He put his hand on his forehead in deep thought.

As if a shot of adrenaline hit him in the face, Steven's head shoots back and his arms come up! *"I got it!"*

We all lean back, a little startled by his response.

"Finish this statement for me, 'It's not what you know it's...'" He waited on our response

In unison the whole group responded quickly, *"It's who you know!"* as though that was the easiest question he could have asked us.

Even I had heard that quote multiple times. I hope he is coming with advice stronger than that!

Straight away he made a sound like the buzzer you hear in NBA and hockey games, *"errrrrrrnt. WRONG."*

Everyone looks at each other, wrong? How can we be wrong?

Steven starts laughing, obviously amused by our reactions. I am selfishily happy I'm not the odd one out on this one, as I have been with all the other information today.

Steven interrupts our confused looks, *"When I was in undergrad I thought the same thing, 'It's not what you know, it's who you know'. I have heard it preached at different leadership workshops; I have read it in a few books; I have even seen it so much that I believed it. That was until I got into the real world and my view was corrected."*

❝ *It's not what you k̶n̶o̶w̶, it's who you know* **❞**

"What's the power of knowing someone if they don't know you?" Steven asks the group.

No-one answers.

"Exactly. There is no power," he continues. *"You knowing who the Queen of England is or your town mayor, only benefits you if they know who you are.*

"The true statement is, 'It's not who you know, it's what you know and who knows you.'"

❝ *It's not who you know, it's what you know and who knows you.* **❞**

"What changed your view?" said Zach, Head of Campus Athletics Association

"As you all know, well everyone except for you Aiden," he said, looking at me, *"when I graduated I attempted to start a company to help freshmen students get acclimated to the college environment, like a mentorship program. I decided I was going to commit the whole summer after graduation to advertising my company to incoming parents and students."*

"How did it go?" I asked.

"It failed. My goal was to get 100 parents to pay for this program for their kid. You know how many parents signed up?"

"How many?"

"Only 1!" he responds. *"O N E, as in Numero UNO! So unfortunately, I had to jump into the corporate world."*

He continues.

"But the story doesn't end there. During that summer I decided I wanted to get good tickets to see my favorite musician, so that meant standing in a long line for multiple hours. I stood in line for a little over 4 hours one Saturday! Not sure if any of you have ever stood in line for multiple hours, but you tend to make friends with the people you are standing alongside."

Everyone nods their head as though they can relate. I can definitely relate, as I have stood in line for much longer than 4 hours!

He continues, *"We held each others spots while each other took bathroom breaks, got food, and took important phone calls. We also had great conversation and got to know each other during those hours. Who knew those conversations would pay off?*

"During the last hour, me and a lady I was standing next to in line started chatting about where we went to school and what we did for a living. It turned out that she got both her Bachelor's and her MBA degree from Myatt University. We not only had the musician in common, but we now had our alma mater and the same undergraduate major!

"She started telling me about the company she worked for, which happened to be a huge employer in the area! Since I only had one parent signed up at the time, I knew there was a chance I might not have a business come the start of the school year so I asked for her business card, just in case."

"I hope this story is leading somewhere good," says Zach.

"Yes it is, give me a moment, we're getting there," responds Steven as he contines his story.

"I told her that if the business didn't work out I would reach out to her to see if there were any opportunities at the company she worked.

"So, let's fast forward about two months. The business didn't work out and I was now an employee at a bank, which was the fastest job I could get after realizing I needed money for food and bills, and the business wasn't going to provide it. This job was not where the lady from the concert line worked, I found this job on my own."

"Did you have a job during that summer?" says Imani.

"Well, I had a job for part of the summer and then I made the mistake of quitting to focus solely on the business fulltime. That was only ONE of the mistakes I made that summer," says Steven.

Everyone laughs.

"After a few months at the bank, I decided I wanted a change of environment and felt with all I accomplished in college I deserved a little more money and a better position. I decided to apply for a position at the financial firm where the lady I met at the concert worked. I was confident in my resume and skills so I decided to apply without contacting the lady I met.

"You had her info and you didn't ask for help when you first applied?" I asked.

"Yup, didn't think I needed it" replied Steven

"Now I have no doubt all of you will have great resumes when you graduate because you are all involved and making an impact. I believed that with my internships, GPA, and extra curricular activities I would at least get an interview for the position.

"I was WRONG."

"You didn't even get an interview with all you did during college? You were Student Body President," says Imani, looking shocked.

"I know, I guess that meant nothing to HR," Steven says while chuckling.

⏰ **WAKING UP CHASE** ⏰

"I want you all to remember the number 4. As I look back at what occurred, the number 4 is important," says Steven with a focused look.

"It's important because I waited in line for tickets for a little over 4 hours. The number 4 becomes even more important as we continue."

He pauses.

"After applying by myself at the financial firm, it took 4 weeks for me to receive my denial email from Human Resources."

"How long did I wait in line with the lady?" Steven asks the group.

"4 hours," we respond.

".... And how many weeks did it take for me to get denied by HR without her help," he asks.

"4 weeks," we respond again.

"Good, I wanted to make sure y'all were paying attention," he says.

"For me, that was the first time my resume didn't get me where I assumed it would. I knew I would at least get an interview." Steven stresses the two words **at least!**

"But guess what, the story didn't end there," he says leaning in... *"Because what did I still have at my disposal?"* he asks, looking at everybody around the table.

"That lady's business card?" says Zach.

"Right! I pulled out her business card and happened to notice something I didn't notice earlier. The lady's position was Director at the financial firm. She wasn't a Director in the department in which I was applying, but she was fairly high up in the company.

"Lesson number one of this story. Somebody might have on plain clothes, and look 'regular' per se, but you never know who they are. That goes back to never judging a book by its cover!

> **"** *Never judge a book by its cover. Unless you read it before that is, then it's perfectly ok to judge.* **"**

"After not being able to get the job based on my resume alone, I took out her business card and emailed "The Director." I let her know I applied for a position and was denied, I then asked if she could help, to which she graciously agreed."

I look around to see everyone's eyes fixed on Steven, waiting to hear what happened. I laugh inside as I see our bodies are all leaning forward as though our lives depend on every word.

"Alright," he says. *"Remember it took me 4 weeks to get my denial email back from HR?"* He waits for us to show agreement.

"Well check this," he said with a smile, knowing he was about to give the hook to the story. *"After I emailed 'The Director' it took only 4 hours to get an email back from HR with an interview date. One email from*

'The Director' to HR got me an interview. The only reason why I know the timeframes is because I was amazed at how fast I received a response."

It looks like someone's turned on lights in a completely dark room as all our faces light up with the AH-HA moment.

"You received a response back in just 4 hours?" I ask, making sure I heard the last number right.

"Yes," Steven responded. *"By myself it took four weeks to get denied, with 'The Director's' email, it took 4 hours to get an interview!"*

"She got you an interview that quick?" I ask again.

"Yes, she did. Right there lies the power of someone KNOWing and trusting YOU. Catch this, me knowing her would have not been of benefit if she didn't know who I was.

"Here's what's even better about this story, I started at the company a few months later with a 10k raise compared to my previous job at the bank."

"10k as in $10,000?" asks Imani.

"Yes," Steven confirms.

"This story is important because it illustrates the importance of people knowing who you are. It illustrates the importance of building relationships so you are able to call on people you know when you need assistance. I want you to realize that if she didn't know who I was, me just knowing her would have been of no help."

"I noticed you kept the 'What you know,' inside the quote. You didn't get rid of it," says Zach.

"Good point. I did keep it in because 'The Director' could only get me the interview. I had to sell myself to get the job and once I was hired I also had to do the job well. Me knowing 'The Director' only got me in the doorway, it didn't allow me a seat inside.

> ❝ *KNOWING SOMEONE keeps you ringing the doorbell; Someone KNOWING YOU opens the door; WHAT YOU KNOW allows you a seat inside.* ❞

"We all know of different celebrities, politicians, and other people who are famous, but how many of them know you? If you needed one of them, how many of you can get on the phone with them right now?"

Steven answers his own question. *"None of us at this point in our lives.*

"It's not who you know, it's who knows YOU. Your success in school and post undergrad years will be determined by how many relationships you foster and how many people can vouch for you and your work. She took a risk on recommending me only after being around me for four hours, which means I made a good impression.

"Just knowing her would have done me no good, but her knowing and trusting me made all the difference. Your resume can only take you so far.

"Aiden, Linda showed you the blank piece of paper this morning, right?"

"Right," I say.

"That paper can only take you so far. You have to put time into establishing relationships with individuals in those organizations on that paper. After I first met 'The Director' in line for tickets, I emailed her immediately upon returning home to thank her for the conversation and enjoyable time that day. My email strengthened and built upon those four hours we had spent together earlier. The email pushed the relationship even further.

"The worst time to check up on someone is when you need their assistance with something. You want to cultivate your relationships, so when assistance is needed, they know you care and are more than willing to help"

> **"** *The worst time to check up on someone is when you need them.* **"**

"Aiden, your resume will be full when you leave here in a few years, but don't start joining a bunch of organizations just to fill it up. Make sure you are actually adding value to what you join. Make sure you're a good leader, make sure people respect you and want to be a part of your vision. Your name and people's perception of you will always last longer than that resume you will hold."

> **"** *People will often forget what you did, but they will never forget how you made them feel.* **"**
> Maya Angelou

"Dang, that's crazy how one 4 hour encounter increased your salary by $10,000! So one relationship was worth 10k to you?"

asks Bryan.

"Great way to think about it," says Steven.

"That ONE relationship was worth 10k to me. But there's more…A year later, a friend I met my first night of Freshmen Orientation and kept in contact with over the years recommended me for a position at the consulting company I work for now. That raise was another 7k in total; those two relationships were worth $17,000 to me. Both of those jobs happened because two people who knew ME decided to make one phone call or send an email.

"Here's the question for all of you leaders at this table, who will be a part of your 17k relationships? What relationships have you built or will build that will allow you to pick up the telephone and make something happen? Who trusts you that much?"

REFLECTION

Who will be a part of your 17k relationships? What relationships have you built or will build that will allow you to prosper?

He pauses as we all ponder our personal lists of friends and classmates. Everyone is silent, all in deep thought.

Steven lets us dwell for a moment and then continues on.

"I went through college thinking after undergrad my resume would get me anywhere I needed because I busted my ass. When y'all get out you're competing against those students who also busted their ass during their four years. You have it wrong if you think you're only competing against the non-achieving 2.0'ers," he says with a smirk.

"....aaaannnd that is when the relationship factor comes in. In fact, it was the relationships I built while in those organizations and on campus which were truly valuable post graduation."

Chase chimes in, *"Not sure why I never considered the true importance of relationship building until I heard your story. Luckily, I've established some great relationships on and off campus, but it's great to understand how much it really matters."*

"See Aiden, you're lucky" says Chase, looking first at me and then around at the Cabinet. *"We are getting this information fairly late in the game, luckily you have a few years to put this into practice."*

"You're right," I say, nodding my head, *"Thanks for sharing, Steven."*

I looked back at all my relationships made thus far; I wasn't involved on campus so I didn't have many to look back on. Though I could never predict what would become of my current friends, I had to ask myself if they were likely to become a part of my 17k relationships? My answer was clear, more than likely, no.

"That's exactly why I love spending time with you all because I always come away knowing more and feeling inspired," says Chase, interrupting my private thoughts.

"I feel the exact same way, it goes back to the importance of surrounding yourself with good people," says Imani.

"We could go on for hours," Chase says, looking down at his watch, *"but there's still one person we have to meet with before our day together ends."*

"Who's next?" asks Bryan.

"Reagan," says Chase, smiling and looking over at her, seated next to Bryan.

"Ohhhhhh, Reagan gets private time and we don't huh? It must be because of those Student Body President Powers she has."

Everyone laughed.

"I'll let you know when I get those powers," says Reagan as everyone starts to rise from their seats.

⏰ **WAKING UP CHASE** ⏰

"*It was nice meeting you all. Thanks for spending this time with me today and laying down the knowledge! I'll have to spend tonight going through all my notes and everything y'all said,*" I say, looking at The Cabinet.

"*You're welcome,*" says Zach. "*We threw a lot of information at you, I was very impressed to see you taking notes throughout. Make sure you review your notes tonight to ensure you don't lose a lot of what we talked about.*"

"*And be sure to reach out to any of us if you want clarification on anything*" says Steven as he starts writing his number on my notes sheet in the bottom right corner. Zach follows suit, quickly followed by Imani and the the others, until everyone has written their phone numbers on my notepaper. I let them continue writing, knowing I will never get the opportunity to contact them.

"*.... Hey Chase!*" says Imani, causing both our heads to turn. "*Bring the kid to the next event, ok?*" referring to me as she heads out the room.

"*Yeah, sure*" says Chase, not knowing for sure how long I would be with him.

Everyone says their goodbyes along with a hug until only Reagan, Chase and I are left.

"*Aiden, you haven't mentioned food since you walked in here. What happened?*" he says, laughing as the door shuts behind the last person.

"*You're right!*" I say, considering how I'd totally forgotten about hunger once we started talking. "*I guess you can be filled in other ways, huh?*"

"*Exactly,*" says Chase. "*And then there were three,*" *he added,* looking at Reagan and me.

"*Three there is,*" says Reagan *as* we walk out of the private dining room. "*You want to head over to my office?*"

"*You have an office?*" I ask.

"*Yeah, Student Body President and Vice President have offices on campus,*" says Reagan.

"*So that means you have an office too,*" I say, looking at Chase.

"*Yup,*" he says. Leaning closer to me, he whispers, "*We have an office,*" as we both chuckle.

⏰ **WAKING UP CHASE** ⏰

CHAPTER

17 DEBRIEF

"**W**hat was your biggest takeaway from The Cabinet meeting?" Chase asks as we take our seats in front of Reagan's desk.

"*It would have to be what Imani said about personal responsibility.*"

"*What about it specifically?*" he asks.

"*The idea that I should take responsibility for everything that happens in my life and I'm the blame for everything that occurs. I love it because it leaves no room for second-guessing, it uses the word EVERYTHING, which leaves nothing to chance!*" I continue.

"*I can think of multiple situations that happened in the past week when I quickly shifted blame to someone or something else, when I should have taken responsibility. In the past this mindset has left me sad and even depressed at times. I realize by blaming others it puts me in the position of not having any control to change my situation. To use Imani's words, I was living in the 'Victim stage,' which is a very dark place.*"

Reagan speaks up. "*You're right Aiden, it is a dark place. Quick question, did you happen to notice the energy in the room when you were with The Cabinet?*"

"Actually, I did," I say, surprised she was aware. *"I immediately felt the energy, as everyone's energy radiated from him or her…and I'm not over-exaggerating, I felt it!"*

"Exactly," says Reagan. *"I'm glad the energy was palpable. When I walk around campus, people often ask me if I'm on something!"* she laughs.

'On something like…drugs?" I ask with a confused look.

"Yeah," says Reagan.

"People don't ask me that," says Chase, *"but people do ask me why I'm always so happy and positive."*

Reagan continues, *"A lot of that positive energy shines through because I don't let anyone or any situation get in the way of my happiness and place me in the Victim Stage. As soon as something that can be perceived as negative occurs, I immediately take personal responsibility and start brainstorming solutions or fixes. I'm always in control."*

> **❝** *Negative energy flows when you convince yourself don't have control.* **❞**

"Can you imagine what your life would feel like if everything always happened to you? Of course you would be walking around with a grey cloud over your head!" says Reagan.

"I agree," says Chase.

"Is it hard to maintain that mindset everyday?" I ask.

"To be honest, most things are hard when you first start, but the more you do anything the easier it becomes. All of these things will become second nature and you'll start doing them without even thinking. Treat every principle you learned today as though it's a muscle, in order for a muscle to grow what has to happen Aiden?"

"You have to work it out?" I respond.

"Yes, and the muscle has to tear! Your muscles have to tear for the true growth to occur. There's going to be moments when you feel 100% that something is not your fault. Your growth or the tearing of your muscles will occur in those moments. Remember to take responsibility, re-evaluate, and come up with a solution."

"I'm ready for the tearing," I say, looking at Chase and Reagan.

"You'll certaintly get some opportunites to practice," says Reagan.

CHASE TIP

You have an opportunity in every situation to take responsibility, which allows you to be in control of your destiny. Don't allow any situation or individual to convince you differently.

⏰ **WAKING UP CHASE** ⏰

— PART —

5

MEETING WITH THE PRESIDENT

THE SILENT KILLER

"*I can say with full confidence that I saved the best for last,*" says Chase.

"*Stop it,*" says Reagan as she blushes.

"*I'm serious,*" says Chase, turning to look at me, "*Reagan's story is a great example of what it takes to be successful on campus, and if you capture what she says, not only will your next few years be better, but your whole life will be as well.*"

I sit up in my seat, interested to hear more.

Chase continues, "*Aiden, do you want to know what I hate?*" He pauses, not waiting long enough for me to respond.

"*Now, I don't hate many things, but what we are about to discuss is my enemy, my arch nemesis, the Joker to my Batman. I absolutely hate this thing!*"

"*Absolutely?*" I say sarcastically. "*What is it?*" I ask, a little more interested now after his description.

"*Before I tell you what it is, I want to tell you why I hate it. I hate it because it is the one thing that has stopped most people from achieving what they want to accomplish.*

"I hate it because every year it kills millions of people. It kills their ideas, dreams, potential and everything else in their path. To be perfectly honest, it harms more people than cancer does every year.

"I hate it because it is one of the few diseases we are all born with, yet there's no easy cure. It's something that most people ignore because the disease convinces you of things that are not true, but over time we start to believe it."

"Seriously Chase, what is it?" I ask impatiently.

"Alright, I won't make you wait any longer, the disease I've been describing is…

"FEAR, Aiden."

"Fear as in being afraid, right?" I ask, thinking it was something bigger.

"Yes fear. Every day fear harms the world, yet the world doesn't actively work towards a cure. If we can get you to understand this disease can be conquered, then today was a success," says Chase.

"So the success of today relies on this ONE lesson?" I ask with a concerned laugh.

"Yes, this is the foundation to it all, which is why he saved me for last," says Reagan with a smile. ☺

"I wanted you to meet with Reagan because she's a prime example of what taking fear head on can do for your life. I also love when she shares her story, so I couldn't let the day end without you hearing it."

"You flatter me," she says to Chase.

Reagan continues, *"I agree with Chase, Aiden. Too many students walk across the graduation stage every year, never once getting close to all they could have accomplished during their time on campus."*

"Are you saying that is mainly because of fear?"

"Exactly," says Reagan.

Reagan then says something that totally throws me for a loop

"Graduation can be compared to Death," says Reagan.

"Death?" I ask.

Taking it a little far, huh? I think as she attempts to explain further.

"Work with me," she says. *"When you graduate, all your dreams you had during your four years, like leaving a legacy, studying abroad, going Greek, running for a certain office, all of that dies with you if you don't make it happen during your undergrad years. Once those four years are over, there is no going back."*

She continues,

"Some say, there is always Grad School, but if you have ever chatted with anybody in or out of Grad School, you understand you only get to do undergrad once.

"All of those unmet thoughts and aspirations you had as a bright-eyed freshman die inside of you when you walk across the stage if they

are not fulfilled. Graduation is a happy time, but I shed a few tears every year as I realize with graduation comes the death of many dreams and accomplishments that were never fulfilled."

> **"** *All of those unmet thoughts and aspirations you had as a bright-eyed freshman die inside of you when you walk across the stage if they are not fulfilled.* **"**

"Why were they not fulfilled?" Chase asks as he looks at me. *"I'm glad you asked,"* he says, answering his own question.

"Well, Fear of failure is the biggest. Everyone wants to be successful, but most are not willing to fail their way to success. They never realize that failing is a part of the process; you have to fail at some things in order to get to your ultimate goal. Most avoid trying anything they might fail at because they are so afraid of being judged; therefore they never try in the first place, leaving them unfulfilled."

> **"** *Most avoid trying anything they might fail at because they're so afraid of being judged, therefore they never try in the first place.* **"**

"Were y'all afraid to run for student body office?" I ask them both.

"Yes!" they both say in unison, while nodding their heads vigorously.

 WAKING UP CHASE

"Let me explain what happened to me," says Reagan. Coming into college I knew I wanted to be heavily involved, I just didn't know in what way, so I jumped in full force all around campus. I did well, but I always felt something was missing. I was involved in so many activities to fill a void which couldn't be filled by joining more and more activities.

"It could be compared to having sex with someone to fill the void of never feeling like you were loved during childhood. That's an extreme example, but you get the point."

"Actually, I don't," I say, raising one eyebrow. She's good with these extreme examples, I think to myself. First death, and now sex...dang!

She continues her example,

"Sex will never fill that void, only love will. No matter how many times you have sex, if you never receive the love you're still left by yourself, naked, feeling empty with a half watched Netflix movie."

We all laugh.

"Netflix and...what?" I say to Chase jokingly as they both say *"Chillllll!"* Chase and I continue laughing at her metaphor from total left field.

Reagan continues, *"That's how I felt regarding my extra-curricular involvement. Sophomore year I was asked by a well respected student leader within Student Government if I would run alongside him as he ran for Student Body President. He was going into his senior year, which would leave me open to run for President my following year.*

"When he first asked, I was terrified. We happened to be in a coffee shop on campus at the time, and like every coffee shop you know there was music playing in the background. When he asked me, it felt like the music stopped and I actually wondered if he could hear my heart beating out of my chest.

"See, what my running mate didn't know was that all throughout high school I wanted to run for Student Body Office, I always imagined myself in that type of position, but I let fear win. I let the voice that said 'you're not popular enough' or 'what if you lose?' come into my mind and defeat me, before I even had a chance to fight back.

"That's why it's important to always stand guard at the door of your mind so you are prepared for any attack that may come your way."

Reagan continues passionately, as though she is preaching!

"It's important for those around you to be uplifting, it's important to ignore negative media influences, and it's important to watch the words you say to yourself."

"Amen," I say in agreeance.

She continues, *"I'll never know what ways I could have changed my high school for the better, but I do know those dreams and possible accomplishments died when I walked across that stage at graduation.*

"*What my potential running mate didn't know in that coffee shop that day was that the same negative voice I heard in high school came back again. Because I listened to it last time, this time the voice was a bit louder, and a little more intimidating.*

"It said stuff like... 'Yes, you're involved on campus, but what makes you qualified? You are going to have to debate; you know you've always been afraid of debating. When you lose, the whole campus around you will know you as that girl who lost.' Take note Aiden; the voice didn't even give me a chance to win. The voice said 'WHEN' you lose, not 'if,' but WHEN!

"When the voice of fear speaks, it comes a blazin' because it doesn't want to give you even the slightest chance of thinking something positive could be on the other side.

"Aiden, at all times you will have two voices talking to you; the voice of your potential and the voice of fear. Your fearful voice blocks and entangles the message coming from the voice of your potential.

"Here's the thing: the voice of fear doesn't have all bad intentions, at the end of the day its goal is to protect you. The voice of fear is like Chemothearpy, doing its best to protect you from danger while killing off good cells in the process."

"Protect me from what?" I ask.

"The voice is trying to protect you from the hurt of potential failure or disappointment, which could occur if you fail along the way. The voice of fear doesn't understand that by trying to protect you with potential negative thoughts of what could occur, that it's actually harming you if you decide not to act at all.

"Similar to Chemotherapy, the medicine is needed to make you healthy again, but in the process of killing off what's harming you, it kills off some of the good stuff, making you sick and stagnant at times."

"It's your job to calm that voice and let it know, in the words of Kendrick Lamar that, 'We gone be alright!'" says Chase as we chuckle.

"So, back to the story," says Reagan. *"The voice started to tell me anything possible to get me not to run and to stay in my comfort zone. As I said earlier, trying to protect me from potential pain if I were to lose.*

> **❝** *Your comfort zone is the most dangerous place to reside, either you're growing or you're dying. There is no in between.* **❞**

"I almost convinced myself not to run, until I consulted with The Cabinet and my family. They reminded me of what I was made of and who I was. This goes back to what you learned earlier about the people with whom you surround yourself. You want to have a good defense team, so when the voice of fear starts talking, you have a defense team to back you up. I have nothing against public defenders, but if I'm in trouble I want an All star legal team.

> **❝** *Create a good defense team, so when the voice of fear starts talking, you have a team to back you up. You don't want a team of public defenders.* **❞**

"So after talking it over with my team, I decided to run. We put up posters, handed out fliers and campaigned all around campus. We debated our opponents, and completed all the other tasks it took to run a successful campaign.

"Then the day came when it was time to announce the winners.

"The great news is we broke school records with voting turnout, making it the largest election in school history.

"The bad news is, we lost by just 19 votes."

"Just 19 votes?" I ask in disbelief.

"Yes," says Reagan, *"as in 20 minus 1 equals 19!*

"Aiden, here's what I want you to remember from all of this. Everything the voice of fear tried to convince me of to not run was a lie. All of it was untrue."

"For example?" I ask.

"The voice said 'with a campus as large as Myatt University, if you lose you will never be able to show your face again because everyone will think you are a loser.' When I did show my face a few hours after losing, people were giving me high fives and congratulating me on a good run.

"The voice tried to scare me by convincing me I would be awful in a debate. I did well and no one could tell I was terrified and that it was my first time.

"The voice told me I wasn't qualified to run, but as I visited different organizations during the campaign I realized I was MORE than qualified to run.

"Aiden, what are those things the voice of fear is telling you that aren't true?

REFLECTION

What is the voice of fear telling you that is false? It can be about your academics, leadership abilities, or your potential. What is it for you?

"Is there a certain organization you need to join, is there a certain problem on campus you need to tackle, is there a certain position you need to run for?

"Here's a big one," she continues. *"Are you in the right major or are you majoring in something based on future income alone and not on passion?"*

"Hmmmm," I say out loud, thinking about all the things the voice of fear was stopping me from accomplishing in my life.

"Do you know what the letters in FEAR stand for?" Chase asks.

"No," I reply.

"FEAR stands for False Evidence Appearing Real."

"Consider all the evidence fear gave Reagan not to run and she still decided to run anyway. As she just explained, she lost the election and realized the <u>false evidence</u> fear was providing <u>appeared real</u>, but <u>wasn't real</u>, it was all lies. But she took responsibility for her loss, used the next year to continue to foster great relationships on campus, and ran the following year to now be sitting in front of you as Student Body President."

F *ALSE*

E *VIDENCE*

A *PPEARING*

R *EAL*

"Well done," I say, giving Reagan a few snaps.

"Thanks," says Reagan. *"Aiden, it's never over after a loss or defeat, it's actually just getting started. Change your mindset. If you believed running the first time was difficult with the voice of fear, can you imagine what the voice sounded like the second year when it started yelling 'you're going to lose a second time, don't do it!!'"* she screamed.

We laugh, as she continues.

"I still pushed through that loud voice and listened to that small voice which reminded me of who I was."

> **❝** *Your success is determined by how well you can ignore the loud voice, while listening carefully to the small.* **❞**

Chase adds, *"I wanted you to hear Reagan's story because she is constantly tearing the muscle of fearlessness. The muscle can always become stronger, and she's flexed it hard these past four years. And I can't find a better example of someone who has not only accomplished so much, but shares her story with so much vulnerability."*

He continues,

"Aiden, you can have your plan laid out on what you want to accomplish, like Linda talked about earlier.

"You can have a great mindset and take responsibility for all your actions like Imani talked about.

"You can also form great relationships with those around you like Steven taught us today. But let me be clear when I say none of that matters if you can't conquer your inner self-doubt.

"I didn't realize I wasn't alone in doubting myself until I started listening to a daily Podcast. The creator asked every guest who happens to be a known success, what was the ONE thing holding them back from becoming the person they are today? The answer 99% of the time was their fears and self-doubt.

"Everyone deals with it, but it's those that push through their fears who ultimately leave the legacy on their campus for years to come."

I look over to Chase and Reagan. *"You're saying there's no way to get rid of fear, but over time I can get better at ignoring the voice and pushing past it?"*

"Yes, exactly" they both say.

"That sounds good and all, but how do you ignore the voice, what do you do? Any techniques you can share?" I say, looking at both of them

"Here's one of the techniques I got from the book."

 WAKING UP CHASE

Oh, not that book again, I scream inside.

"I remember the first letter of each word by this phrase I made up, People Don't Keep Secrets," said Reagan.

"What does each letter stand for?" I ask.

"P stands for positive self-talk, what I say to myself about me will show up in my life.

"D stands for daily reading of 'Who am I' affirmation as well as my written copy of my goals.

"K stands for keeping my mind clear by avoiding negative news and radio, and exchanging it for uplifting books, songs, and media.

"S stands for surrounding myself with a good defense team who can remind me of who I am."

"What is that 'Who Am I' thing you mentioned?" I ask.

"Give me a moment," she says as she starts going through drawers looking for it. She pulls out a piece of paper. *"Here it is. I read this every morning to remind myself of my commitments and who I am."*

Who am I?

I am a leader
I create my destiny
I'm leaving a legacy
I will push through fear
Because my end is clear

☼ **WAKING UP CHASE** ☼

I'm not your average student
Watch me prove it!

Meet You At The Top!
Meet You At The Top!
Meet You At The Top!
Because the bottom is getting way too crowded!

The "Who am I?" affirmation, was like the bookend of a full day. I finally understood why The Cabinet and Chase were as successful as they were. If they followed everything they said today and read the "Who am I?" affirmation often, how could they not dominate on our campus? How could they not have those contagious attitudes? How could they not all run major organizations on campus?

The answer is simple; they have all of that because they live what they preach.

"Aiden, Aiden!" says Chase, *"come out your trance man!"* as he waves his hand in front of my eyes.

He is right; I am in a trance of sorts, taking in all that I learned throughout the day so as not to forget any of it if I get back.

"Any parting words for Aiden?" Chase asks Reagan.

"Yes," she says, *"over the next few years, if something scares you, do it. Don't let the voice of fear win. A few years from now I expect you'll be having this same conversation, possibly in this same office with a future student."*

"If not in this office, then at least the one next door," says Chase, signaling to his Vice President's office next door as he laughs.

REFLECTION

What fears are holding you back from succeeding in the future? What would life look like if you pushed through those fears?

— PART —

6

CONCLUSION

CHAPTER 19 THE FINAL WALK

"*W*hat a packed day, Aiden,*" says Chase, as he throws his left arm around Aiden's shoulders, glad to finally be able to talk to him one-on-one again.

"Yeah, you're right man," I say.

"I would have never guessed when I woke up this morning that my day would be spent mentoring my past self about how I did it," says Chase.

"Well, I never would have guessed my day would be spent four years into my potential future, with my potential self," I say, as we both laugh.

"This day was particularly important to me," says Chase, *"because I remember being exactly where you are now. I remember the feelings of doubt and mediocrity. I recall convincing myself that it was ok to be average. Partly, because I believed it, and my surroundings reinforced those beliefs. Also what I said to myself daily, by what I watched and listened to, and my friends – it all played a role in my mediocrity."*

He continues talking as we walk through a now quieting campus as the day comes to an end.

"You've been given a second chance. You've been given the opportunity to see what's possible clearer than most people will ever see. Three years ago,

everything I did, I did based on the faith alone that everything would work out; you now have the strategies, and today I provided the vision for you to see what's possible.

"Do you remember what I said earlier about potential and application Aiden??"

"Yeah," I say. *"You said you are my potential and not a promise. Everything I experienced and learned today will only occur if I apply what I learned."*

> **❝** *Inspiration without application is useless.* **❞**

"You are 100% correct," he says. *"Everything you experienced today is yours and is up for grabs. The energy, passion, and the leaving of a legacy is all up for grabs. If you leave today feeling inspired without applying, today was a waste."*

CHASE TIP

If you don't apply what you're learning from my story, it's a waste. Applying these lessons in your life is key to your future success.

"You're in the middle of your first semester right?" he asks as we get in his vehicle and he starts the car.

"Yeah, just finished mid-terms," I say.

 WAKING UP CHASE 🕐

"Well, now is the time to start, the earlier the better. You got a head start today by discovering all this knowledge in your freshman year, but not everyone gets the same opportunity. Either way, it's never too late to start making a shift when you're off track; it's never too late to start.

> **"** *It's never too late to start making a shift when you're off track; it's never too late to start.* **"**

"Life will not be perfect for you just because you had this experience. You are sure to have some moments of defeat and times when you doubt if everything will come together for the good.

"Remember, you can't connect the dots of life forward, only backwards. You'll get frustrated trying to figure out how life's current situations will connect in the future, when it's impossible to predict in the moment."

"When that moment comes, consider a time you struggled in the past and remember how it didn't make sense back then, but it always came together. We all have those moments when we had no idea how we were going to get through something, but looking back now, you know exactly why that moment happened and you can explain how it made you the person you are today. Right?"

"Yeah, you're right, it always makes sense later on, it just sucks in the moment," I respond.

"Don't get frustrated trying to determine if the dots will connect in the future, the dots will ALWAYS connect in the future, just like they have in the past."

> **"** *You can't connect the dots looking forward; you can only connect them looking backwards. So you have to trust that the dots will somehow connect in your future.* **"**
>
> Steve Jobs

CHAPTER
20 GOODBYES

Just as he finishes his sentence, we pull up to the place it all started.

The place I woke up to this morning, bewildered, confused, and not sure where the day would take me.

It was now dusk and we knew it was the end.

We exit the car, with Chase meeting me as I step on the sidewalk. The feeling in the air is apparent as we both realize this might indeed be the end. We understand there is a possibility we will never see each other again in this form.

We both know there will be no one else in the world that understands our lives better than we understand each other right now.

"I'm so proud of you Chase," he says to me as he reaches out for a hug, his voice a little shaky.

"I'm proud of you too, Chase!" I say back, as some random liquid forms in my eyes – I cough and wipe it before Chase notices.

"Meet you at the top?" he says with a laugh, reaching out his hand for a handshake.

"Yeah.....meet you at the top man!" I say back, shaking his hand as I turn around and head towards the building. As the car drives off I watch it drive off until it can't be seen any longer.

As I head back upstairs, I feel drained and filled all at the same time from today's festivities. To say I am tired would be the understatement of the year! As I put my keys in the door and walk in the room, I'm so happy to not see Mason there. I'm done talking for the day and since I can't put today into words right now, I don't want to attempt to tonight.

I throw my shoes off and jump on the bed, ready to chill for the night. I take out my notes from the day and scan them, realizing if this was a dream I won't be able to take them with me. I finish my review as I promised Steven I would, and place the notes in my pocket.

My intent was to lounge and watch television until Mason ultimately got back, but my body didn't agree. As quickly as I entered this unfamiliar world, I left it at the same speed as I drifted off to sleep.

CHAPTER 21 WAKING UP CHASE

"*Bruh, wake up!*" I hear as a pillow crashes down on my torso!

My head's pounding. Braden's talking. Uhhhhh, this hangover sucks.

Wait? I ask myself.

Braden talking?

Hangover?

I quickly pull the covers back to see my room and Braden in the process of picking up another pillow to throw.

"*YESSSS!!*" I yell, as he looks at me with confusion

"*Are you ok?*" he asks, putting down the pillow.

"*Besides this headache, I'm great!*" I respond with an enthusiasm he's never seen before.

"*It's 10am, you've already missed your 9am. I told you it wasn't a good idea to go out last night.*"

"*Yeah, yeah, yeah,*" I say, "*I knowwww, I learned my lesson.*"

Almost as soon as the word lesson comes from my mouth I quickly remember, MY NOTES! I frantically start checking my pockets…

Left Front – nothing

Right Front – nothing

Wait, I think. Did I put them in my back pocket? I'm sure I put them in my front.

I check both back pockets to find nothing. Damn, it was a dream. But…it just felt so real I think in dismay.

I jump up, go to my desk and immediately write down a few reminders from my experience.

Plan early, leave empty, take responsibility, surround yourself with good people, live fearlessly. Am I missing anything I think frantically? I decide to stop for now and see if I can remember anything post hangover.

"What's up with you man?" asks Braden.

"Just writing down some things someone told me at the party last night," I quickly lie so as to not sound as crazy as I'd been acting the past few minutes.

Even though I am recovering from what was sure to have been an epic night, I feel extremely positive about the day and what is next for my future.

WAKING UP CHASE

I reach underneath a few papers on my desk and grab the book given to all students upon entering Myatt.

I open it up to the front section and read the words again "If you don't read this once it's given you, if you don't apply what's within the story will become you"…. Trying to make some sense of what occurred in my dream.

"Hey Braden, you read this, right?"

"Yes, I've been telling you to read it since we got here," he says in a frustrated tone.

"So what is it about?" I ask, scared about what the answer may be.

"It's about a student who meets someone who helps him see what he was always capable of."

Makes sense, but I'm still confused. Not sure what I drank last night, but I need to stay away from whatever it was!

"I think I'll read it," I say to Braden as he looks at me like I might be sick.

"Are you ok?" he says, as I hear Mason's voice from earlier saying the exact same thing in my head.

"Yes, I'm perfectly fine," I respond. *"Is this the only thing this author wrote that you read?"*

⏰ **WAKING UP CHASE** ⏰

"No, he just released a book that actually teaches you how to apply the principles learned in this book in greater depth." He points to another book laying on a pile of papers on his desk.

I'm about to get some food before my Freshmen Council meeting, you want to grab something with me?" says Braden.

"Yeah, give me a moment." I reply, as I grab my water bottle, put on something presentable, and consider how my reading list is growing by the minute.

CHAPTER
22 END OF THE ROAD

As we walk outside, I can't help but think forward about my day with Older Chase and what the campus will look like in the future. I look around to see the old buildings that were replaced with state of the art facilities in my dream.

"Did you have a good time last night?" Braden asks.

"Uhhhh…I don't remember last night," I say with a laugh.

"With all you consumed, I'm surprised you woke up!"

As Braden finishes his sentence, a familiar face comes into view. It was a face I never noticed on campus previously, but I know exactly who she is now.

"Hey Braden," she says with a smile as she walks closer to us.

"Hey Reagan," Braden responds.

"Reagan, this is my best friend Chase," he says as we shake hands. *"I've been trying to get him to come to the SGA meeting for the longest, one day we'll get him on board, one day!"* We all laugh.

As Braden and Reagan talk I can't help but notice how much younger she looks. The last conversation of my day was with an older presidential Reagan, not this girl in front of me.

"Reagan," I say, interrupting them in conversation, not able to hold out any longer. *"Have you ever considered running for student body office?"* Braden looks at me wondering how I even knew that position existed. It was a selfish question, as I just needed confirmation if my dream had anything to do with reality.

"Naaaa, not really my thing," says Reagan as she starts to continue on her way before she turns to Braden and asks…

"Braden, I'm getting a small group of friends together tonight if you would like to join us."

"Sure," says Braden, *"Do you mind if Chase comes along too?"*

"Uhhh, sure," says Reagan, only agreeing because I am standing there.

Not sure why, but something inside told me her answer regarding her potential presidential endeavor wasn't completely true.

We continue walking for around 5 minutes on our quest for food when we hear a faint voice getting closer and what sounds like someone jogging behind us. We turn around to see Reagan again, breathing hard as though she just finished a sprint.

"Chase?" she says. *"Your name is Chase, right?"* as she tries to catch her breath.

"Yeah, what's up?" I respond.

"As I walked away from you two I saw these on the ground, it looked like someone's notes so I figured I would try to return them when I noticed your name." She hands me a few crumpled sheets of paper. *"I thought you probably dropped them by mistake."*

I look down at the papers with my handwriting throughout the pages.

"Yeah, probably" I say. *"Thanks, I appreciate it Reagan!"* I call after her as she walks away, still catching her breath.

I quickly look through the crumpled papers and notice some familiar notes.

"What's that?" asks Braden, as he watches me read through the pages with a huge smile. ☺

"Nothing important," I say, still looking through the pages in total disbelief

I turn to the second page to notice a few names and phone numbers in the right corner. I take out my phone and dial one of them.

Rinnnggg!
(Silence)

Rinnnggg!
(Silence)

⏰ **WAKING UP CHASE** ⏰

Rinnnggg…
The ringing stops.

"Hello?" says a familiar voice on the other end of the line.

To be continued…

You've read the book to the end, good for you, but application is everything so you still have work to do.

Reading means nothing if you don't apply, if you don't use what's within you could find yourself passed by.

You're now done so be sure to share, for keeping this from other student leaders would be unfair.

AMAZON REVIEW

The biggest thank you can give is an honest review. It is also the best way for others to learn and share the messages within Waking Up Chase.

After placing your review, take a screenshot and send to the email address below so I can show my appreciation with a free surprise gift.

Email: **Info@BellamyInspires.com**
Subject: Amazon Review

Thank you in advance!

MEET THE AUTHOR

Just a few years after earning his bachelor's degree, Darryl Bellamy Jr., has earned kudos as a student success and leadership expert addressing audiences on campuses and at conferences and inspiring his peers to take action. His mandate is - Define Your Experience.

Darryl's accompanying message is to encourage students to overcome self-doubt, set goals, and build robust and lasting relationships on campus in order to excel. His goal is to inspire millions of students to DECIDE what they want, PUSH through fear, and DEFINE their Experience. He knows from personal experience that if students grasp and develop these skills in college, they will be unstoppable come post-graduate life.

Darryl earned his bachelor's degree in Business Management from the University of North Carolina at Charlotte. Darryl held internships with AT&T and SunTrust Bank during college, has worked for two Fortune 100 companies after graduation, and currently serves as the founder of Bellamy Inspires, LLC. He also worked as a Consultant and served as a trainer with a National Leadership Training Co., where he has addressed groups around the nation. Darryl was recently named on New Orleans WUPLTV among the top 10 inspirational Instagram accounts to follow.

Darryl knows the difficulties in balancing a student workload while trying to plan for the future. He strives for each student to leave his programs with boldness to ignore their negative self-talk and start living their college experience on their terms.

ACKNOWLEDGEMENTS

My heartfelt gratitude goes to every person who helped make me the person I am today. I can write a book revolving around your impact in my life. I can't say thank you better.

Parents

I honor your sacrifice above all. Thank you for being supportive and loving parents through all my ideas, those that worked out and the many that did not. I love you both and pray that I continue to make you proud.

Siblings

To say I have the best siblings in the world is an understatement. I have to love you, but I don't have to like you. I can genuinely say I love and like you. You are supportive, understanding, and the best siblings I could ask for. Thank you.

All Reviewers

A Huge thank you to all of you who reviewed the draft and provided feedback. Thanks for your honesty and grammatical jokes! Your support and early reviews are the reason WUC is what it is.

Kendall Allen | Darius Bellamy | Latisha Byrd | Harrison Flood | Quineice Harris | Kyla Jones | Frederick Kenley | Latoya Mackey | Alex Mitchell | Antonio Riggins | Paige Torres

Friends

I believe "You are the average of the people you spend the most time with," and I can say my average is pretty darn high. Thank you to all of you who call, text, email, Facebook message, etc. with support. Thanks for listening when I needed to get out an idea, practice new material, and being by my side for it all.

Past Teachers & Educators & Student Affairs Professionals

A big part of my life is comprised of all the teachers, educators, and professionals I have come into contact with over the past 25 years. I can't say enough about the impact you all have had on my life. You have taught me lessons I will never forget and have given me a special gift - your time. Thank you.

SPEAKING

Darryl's keynote programs and workshops are transparent, entertaining, informative and motivational! He travels around the country speaking on campuses and at conferences spreading his message to students of all ages. Invite Darryl to speak today, the full updated list of programs can be found at www.BellamyInspires.com.

The Fearless Experience: Facing Your Fears to Get Everything You Want Variations: Fearless Student, Fearless Student Leader, Fearless Greek.

The one thing holding most students back from experiencing all campus has to offer is fear. Darryl has collected over a thousand fears from students and uses that research to help student's breakthrough fears to lead on campus and in post-grad life. This program is great for any student group.

The Freshmen Experience: Three Things You Must Do and How to Make Them Happen.

The program uses the lessons learned in 'Waking Up Chase' combined with Darryl's personal stories to keep students enthused. TFE inspires first-year students to know their vision and define their why, understand the importance of building relationships on campus, and how to push through fear to dominate in undergrad.

Custom Program: Have a specific theme for a conference or need another topic? We'll work with your specifications and create a special solution for your event.

SPEAKING TESTIMONIALS

"I can not begin to express how excited, moved and inspired I was by this presentation. Darryl did a phenomenal job."

Mindy Sides –Walsh, *Director of Leadership Development*

"His warmth, compassion, and desire to see other students succeed is fed by an ordained spirit. He has developed superb content, mastered the podium, and engaged students to overcome their fears."

Nicole Greer, *Speaker, Coach & Facilitator*

"This really helped me, fear is something I really struggle with; very helpful"

Student Evaluation

"Darryl Bellamy is the REAL DEAL - He possess an uncanny, natural and infectiously positive nature combined with a wealth of polished skills as a speaker and facilitator."

Eric Rowles, *Owner of Leading to Change*

"Your message was timely and inspiring. Society is in need of more positive voices like yours to penetrate the ears and souls of our young people."

Janice Goldsby, *Assistant Principal*

"He was good at what he did, he brought out emotions in people that were warming"

Student Evaluation

CONNECT WITH DARRYL

I look forward to hearing from you!

Any questions or comments can be sent to Info@bellamyinspires.com or send me a message through any of the social media platforms below.

Newsletter - Sign up for at BellamyInspires.com for updates on relevant topics, youtube videos, and future books.

- Facebook.com/BellamyInspires
- Twitter.com/BellamyInspires
- Instagram.com/BellamyInspires
- SnapChat/BellamyInspires
- YouTube.com/BellamyInspires

Made in the USA
Columbia, SC
09 August 2021